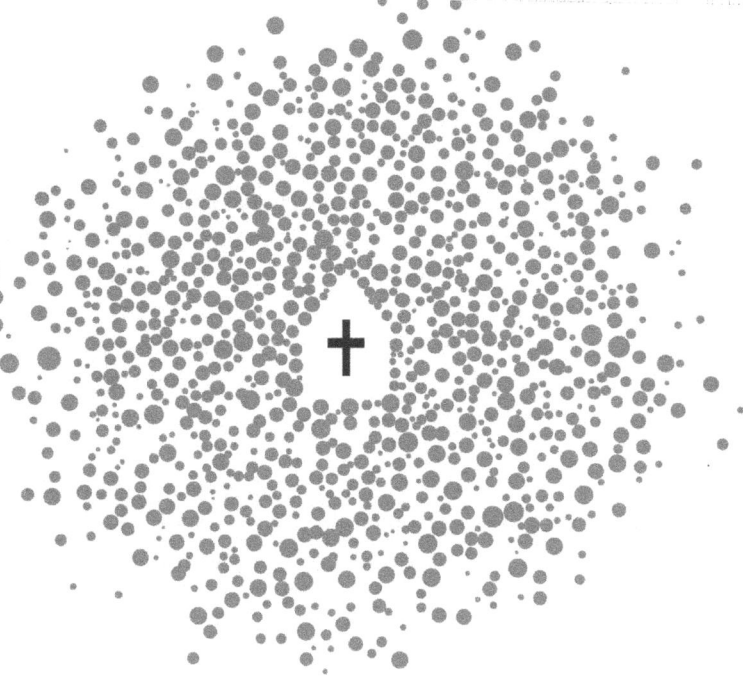

Finding Church

Stories of Leaving, Switching, and Reforming

FINDING CHURCH: STORIES OF LEAVING, SWITCHING, AND REFORMING
Copyright © 2012 by Civitas Press
All rights reserved
ISBN #978-0615710884
Published by Civitas Press, LLC
San Jose, CA,
www.civitaspress.com

Unless otherwise noted, Scripture quotations marked NIV are taken from the Holy Bible, New International Version®. Copyright © 1973, 1978, 1984 by International Bible Society. Used by permission of Zondervan Publishing House. All rights reserved. The "NIV" and "New International Version" trademarks are registered in the United States Patent and Trademark Office by International Bible Society. Use of either trademark requires permission of International Bible Society.

Scripture quotations marked ESV are from The Holy Bible, English Standard Version® (ESV®). Copyright © 2001 by Crossway, a publishing ministry of Good News Publishers. Used by permission. All rights reserved.

Finding Church

STORIES OF LEAVING, SWITCHING, AND REFORMING

Edited by Jeremy Myers

Publishing inspiring and redemptive ideas.℠

For all people who live as the church by being the hands and feet of Jesus.

CONTENTS

Acknowledgments	7
Introduction	8
Section 1 - Leaving Church	14
Chapter 1 - How Seminary Helped Me Leave Church	20
Chapter 2 - My Journey Out of Church	26
Chapter 3 - My Road to Leaving Church	31
Chapter 4 - An Epic Ecclesiastical Adventure	35
Chapter 5 - Janette's Church Crisis	42
Chapter 6 - How Professor P. J. Gomes Helped Me Question Evangelicalism	46
Chapter 7 - A Heretic Among Us	52
Chapter 8 - Leaving Church to Find Church	56
Chapter 9 - Nevertheless	61
Chapter 10 - Following the Gypsy King	67
Chapter 11 - Leaving for Love	72
Chapter 12 - A Recovering Drug Addict	78
Chapter 13 - Leaving Church In the Age of Social Media	83
Section 2 - Switching Church	89
Chapter 14 - Church Change	93
Chapter 15 - From Factory-Farmed God to Grass-Fed Jesus	99
Chapter 16 - What Is "Church," Anyway?	103
Chapter 17 - My Search for A Family	109
Chapter 18 - Urban Missionaries	113
Chapter 19 - One of the Biggest Problems With Church Is Often the Pastor!	121
Chapter 20 - Loyalty	126
Chapter 21 - A Refuge In Times of Trouble	133

Chapter 22 - Looking for the Kingdom	138
Chapter 23 - A Collective Yes	145
Section 3 - Reforming Church	149
Chapter 24 - Being the Change I Want to See	154
Chapter 25 - Love Lost and Found	161
Chapter 26 - The Church Is Messy, but You Can't Live Without Her	165
Chapter 27 - A Story of Becoming	170
Chapter 28 - Being the Change I Want to See	174
Chapter 29 - Part of the Continual Work of Reforming the Church	179
Chapter 30 - The Red Truck Contingency Plan	183
Chapter 31 - The Bride with Holes In Her Dress	187
Chapter 32 - Jumper Cables	191
Chapter 33 - Being On Mission Together	195
Chapter 34 - I Hate the Church. I Love the Church.	201
Chapter 35 - Focusing On People	207
Chapter 36 - We Want Worship!	212
About the Contributors	219

ACKNOWLEDGMENTS

This book never would have been possible without the help and input of thousands of other people. I want thank my parents for raising me up within the church and teaching me the things of God, and my wife's parents for supporting me when few others would. I also thank the scores of people I have served with in the various churches I pastored or attended. You taught me more about church than I could learn in any book.

Several people were also influential in the idea behind this book. Alan Knox was one of the first people who got me thinking in new ways about the church. Frank Viola befriended me online even though we have never met. Kathy Escobar invited me into her church, "The Refuge," and renewed my hope and vision for the church. Sam Riviera has been a faithful and loving friend for more years than we have known.

Most of all, I want to thank my beautiful wife and three daughters. They are my joy, my encouragement, and my inspiration. They are one of the primary reasons I write. I especially thank them for kindly giving me time and space to finish the manuscript of this book while in the middle of moving from New York to Oregon. Neither the book nor the move was easy, but we accomplished both!

Finally, I thank Jonathan Brink of Civitas Press for working with me on this book and being patient with me as I missed deadlines and sent in a manuscript, which is almost certainly full of errors. Thanks for making this book better.

INTRODUCTION

In several hundred years, historians will view the church of twenty-first century the way we view the Reformation church of the sixteenth century. The upheaval and changes taking place in the church today are just as momentous as those that rocked Christianity during the life of John Wycliffe, William Tyndale, Martin Luther, Ulrich Zwingli, and John Calvin.

Numerous factors are contributing to the changes we see today, not least among them being the rise of postmodernism, a threat of nuclear war, an emerging global economy, and the wide scale adoption of social media. Due to these changes, people view themselves and the world in ways that are unprecedented in human history.

As we learn more about other people and cultures, we grow less certain about what have traditionally been the nonnegotiable beliefs, values, and goals of our own culture. As we learn to love people from other parts of the world, we also discover that some of them want to destroy us. Sometimes their hatred is the justifiable consequence of being mistreated and abused by richer and more powerful nations, but other times, the hatred seems fueled by little more than greed and a lust for power. And through this all, due to the internet, television, and social media, people feel more connected with others half a world away, while at the same time, become less connected to their neighbors, coworkers, and families.

Such changes are shaping the world we live in and whether we recognize it or not, such changes affect the church as well.

As these waves of change wash over the church, there are two ways people typically respond. The vast majority of people don't like the change, and try to keep things the way they were. They beg and plead for others to not rock the boat, to maintain the *status quo*, and to just give them what they are used to and comfortable with. Though such an approach allows most of these churches to survive through the period of upheaval, they lose their ability to speak into the lives of others around them. The church continues to exist, but their message becomes irrelevant and uncompelling.

The other approach that some churches take is to change along with society and culture. Such churches see the changes that occur and try to make similar changes in their structure and ministry. The great danger to such an approach is that many of churches who attempt these changes will not survive. Some become almost mirror images of the culture, while others fall into organizational chaos and doctrinal pitfalls.

A few churches will survive, those that keep their eyes fixed on the lighthouse of Jesus Christ, and who successfully navigate the radical and drastic changes that society and culture force upon them. The people who are part of such churches come from all walks of life, and from all types of churches. This book contains some of their stories.

The stories in *Finding Church* do not contain answers for how to successfully navigate the problems and dilemmas that face the church today. This book simply contains the stories of people who are trying to follow Jesus in new directions and new ways that fit the new demands of a shifting and changing culture. These are the people who are not content to maintain the *status quo*, but are *Finding Church* in new ways and forms.

Their stories fall into three broad categories. First are the stories of those who are "Leaving Church." The title is a bit misleading, because they are not actually leaving the church, but are leaving church "as we know it." They would say that they no longer "go to church" because they are trying to "be the church" instead. As such, they are still active and devoted followers of Jesus Christ, but they are seeking to find church outside the four walls of the traditional church. They believe that Jesus is leading them away from institutional Christianity, and into an organic, relational way of being the church to others.

Those who have contributed stories about "Leaving Church" are simply trying to be the church to those they encounter as they live and work in their day-to-day lives.

Then there are those who are "Switching Church." These stories consist of those people who saw that the church they were part of was not going to change, or was changing to slowly, and so they made the painful and difficult decision to switch from one church to another. Though such people are often denigrated by pastors as "church hoppers" the stories in this section of *Finding Church* reveal hearts and minds which are full of love for Jesus and following him wherever he leads. Sometimes, Jesus leads people from one church to another. These stories reveal some of the motivation and reasons behind such changes, and show that ultimately, people who change churches are trying to follow Jesus just as much as those who stay within a church.

Finally, there are stories from those who are "Reforming Church." These are the stories from those who have experienced pain and hardship in a church, but chose to remain. They may have wanted to leave their church or to switch churches, but chose to stay and "be the change" they wanted to see. They chose to stay and try to help reform and mold the church into what they believe God wants, rather than seek greener pastures elsewhere. They recognize that there is no perfect church, and that often, the problems we have in the churches we attend will follow us to other churches also because these problems are often rooted in us, and not in the place we visit or group we attend. By staying and working to reform their church from within, they believe that God will perform an even greater work in their own lives of molding and shaping them into who he wants them to be.

All of these stories exhibit great pain, courage, and faith. If you are a church leader, many of these stories will be similar to the stories of people in your church, and reading the stories within these pages will help you better understand where they are coming from, what has happened to them in other churches, and what questions and concerns they might have about the church they are currently in.

If you have questions about the church you attend, or are trying to find a new way of doing church or being the church, the stories in this book will inspire you to head out in new directions. The first set of stories will challenge you to leave your current church and follow Jesus in unique ways outside of the four walls of traditional Christianity. The second set of stories will help give you the liberty to switch from the current church you attend to another church in town which may be able to help lead you to a deeper place in your walk with Jesus. The third set of stories will encourage you to stay with the church you currently attend so that you remain faithful to that church and help lead this church in the directions God wants it to go.

Some readers may wonder which category I fall into. The truth is that I fall into all three. I have left church, switched churches, and am trying to reform the church. Thankfully, as the editor of this volume, I did not have to pick a category, but allowed myself the freedom to write for all three. Each of the three sections in the book begins with a short narrative of my own experience. This narrative is then followed with short summaries of the chapters that are included in the rest of the section. I hope that as you read my story, and the stories that follow mine, you will be encouraged to take further steps in your journey of *Finding Church.*

One final note. In this book, the word "church" is used in a variety of ways. Some authors use "church" to refer to the people who gather on certain days of the week in certain buildings for certain events such as prayer, instruction, and fellowship. Others refer to "church" in the more universal sense, where it is the people of God who follow Jesus into the world, regardless of when and where (or even if) they gather. As the editor of this volume, I chose not to require the various authors to stick with one definition of church, but to write about "church" in whatever way made sense to them. Hopefully, this will not cause confusion but will help you discover that one of the first steps in *Finding Church* is learning to define it. If the reader is interested, I have previously written a short book on the definition of church, called *Skeleton Church.*

Now, on to the stories...

SECTION 1
LEAVING CHURCH

I never wanted to leave the first church I pastored. I loved the people and I loved the area. Also, I never wanted to be one of those pastors who could use the phrase "in my first church." But I was young and inexperienced. I made a lot of mistakes in budgeting, planning, administration, and other pastoral areas. But some of my "unforgivable sins" were in the area of preaching.

I once preached a wedding sermon based on Genesis 15 where God makes a covenant with Abram. You know the story: Abram kills a bunch of animals so that he and God can walk through the blood together to seal their covenant, but God puts Abram to sleep and walks through alone. I thought this was a great picture of the covenant between a bride and groom, but the heavy imagery of blood and gore may not have been the best choice of wedding texts. The bride's mother was not happy.

Then there was "The Worst Father's Day Sermon Ever" (as one of my elders later called it). I preached about how Job took his family to live in Sodom, and then after his wife got turned into a pillar of salt, ended up committing incest with his daughters. My message to fathers that day was something along the lines of "Don't do this." Good advice, to be sure, but not the best message for Father's Day.

The sermon that did me in, however, was my "Dead Plant Sermon," as my wife likes to call it. The church was struggling in every way a church can struggle, and one Sunday I got frustrated, and equated the church with a dead and dying plant that was up near the pulpit. There were visitors there that day. They never came back.

A few months later, I was gone too. After my dead plant sermon, the biggest tither in the church stopped tithing, and within a few months the church had no money to pay any of the church bills, including my salary. I had to choose between staying at no pay and moving to another church. After two months of no pay and with baby number two on the way, we chose to leave.

This second church was incredible. The people were loving, kind, honest, hard working, supportive, and generous. In many ways, this church was every pastor's dream church. But after only a year and a half, and after months of prayerful consideration and struggling with the decision, I chose to resign. I felt I needed to finish seminary and take an editing job with a non-profit organization in Dallas that I loved and respected. To this day, I still wonder if I made the right decision.

The non-profit organization was focused on teaching others about the grace of God in Jesus Christ. I was involved in all aspects of the ministry, from shipping out orders of books and DVDs, to organizing local and national conferences, and even editing and typesetting their books and newsletters. I loved the ministry, I loved the people I worked with, and I loved what we focused on.

Then they fired me.

I didn't violate any of the standards of employee conduct, or really do anything that was worthy of being fired. Instead, I happened to read some books about some controversial interpretations of hotly debated Bible topics: Topics like seven-day creationism in Genesis 1–2, whether or not certain Old Testament prophecies about Jesus were really about Jesus, and whether or not hell actually existed. Note that I did not change any of my beliefs in these areas. I was just considering them. I was studying them. I was reading books that argued for views contrary to the ones I believed and taught. I was doing what seminary and my boss had been teaching and training me to do: dig, study, search, and discover the truth by asking hard questions. But apparently, I asked a few questions too many.

When the ministry president found out what I was studying, he convened the board, and they terminated my employment. Apparently, the ministry could not have someone work for them who might one day come to hold some beliefs that were at odds with the beliefs of the ministry. When I pointed out that none of the issues I was studying were actually listed in the ministry's doctrinal statement, I was told that the doctrinal statement would be updated to accurately reflect the views of the ministry. I countered that even if they updated the ministry doctrinal statement, I could sign it in good conscience (I told them I would even sign it in blood!), because I had not changed any of my beliefs; I was only reading and studying positions that were contrary to my beliefs. But nothing I said persuaded them to keep me employed. Ultimately, I was told that the real concern was that I *might* change my views, and that since I held such a prominent role in the ministry, my willingness to study alternative beliefs might negatively affect how donors viewed the ministry, and they might stop giving.

That is when I decided to leave "church" for good. It is not that I was hurt so deeply that I never wanted anything to do with church again. No, it was that I loved the church too much to see the power of the Gospel and the teachings of Jesus be squandered on organizational longevity. This is when I realized that many organizations, including many churches, talk a lot about the Gospel but are more interested in making sure their organization still exists in five or ten years. But if the Gospel truly is more important than the organization, then we should be willing to sacrifice the organization for the sake of the Gospel, if necessary. Through much reading, study, thinking, and reflection, I came to the firm conviction that if a local church could best serve the Great Commission of Jesus by selling its building, canceling its programs, and doing away with doctrinal statements, then that church should take such steps boldly and quickly. (I have written about these ideas in my forthcoming book, *Close Your Church for Good*.)

But I was not just critical of the church. I recognized that if a local church should put the Gospel before longevity, I should do the same. I could not ask a local church to do something I myself had not done. So despite my desperate love for the local church, and my desire to use my training and education in a local church setting, I made the hard decision to *stop going to church* so that I could learn to *be the church* in my town, at my job, and wherever Jesus led. I could never ask a local church to sell its building, or cancel its programs if I had not first sacrificed my own career, my own salary, and my own position for the sake of the Gospel. I first wanted to try "at home" what I though the church should do in the world.

Following Jesus in this way has not been easy, and I have received a lot of criticism for my decision. But while there are many things I miss about attending a traditional church, most days I feel that I am closer to Jesus and doing a better job at following him than ever before.

There are millions of people around the world who feel the same way. A few of them have contributed chapters to this book. Some of these contributors had negative church experiences, while others simply wanted to follow Jesus in a more relational and simple way than what they found in a traditional brick-and-mortar church building. Below are summaries of the stories in this section.

CHAPTER SUMMARIES

Lew Ayotte writes about how he left the church in order to find the church—not in a building with clergy and a congregation, but in life lived together with other people. Though he went to seminary, he discovered the most dangerous question of asking "Why?" and how this leads to questioning the purpose and mission of the church.

In a gracious and insightful essay, Carey Crawford writes about how he led his church to become more missional and incarnational in their outlook and ministry. He writes about the changes he made in his own thinking and ministry, and also some of the changes he made in the church he pastored.

Michael Donahoe shares eight of the reservations he had about institutional church and how grappling with these issues led him to see that church is not found in a building, but in all people who are saved by grace and follow Jesus in their day-to-day lives by loving and serving others.

Glenn Hager served in numerous capacities in several types of churches. But after leaving it all behind, he writes about the loneliness and difficulties of trying to follow Jesus into uncharted waters. Here is a story from a former pastor with lots of experiences and knowledge about church, but who has followed Jesus away from traditional church.

Wayne Hobson retells the story of Janette, a single mother of two, and her damaging church experience in Philadelphia with a self-appointed Apostle and his non-denominational deliverance ministry church. Due to what happened to her and her children, Janette has never set foot inside a church again.

Judith Huang writes a touching story about how Harvard Professor P. J. Gomes helped stabilize her faith by challenging and questioning it, but especially by loving students in this pivotal time of their life. Some people go to Harvard to lose their faith; Judith found hers.

Mike Keffer writes about the pain of being condemned as a heretic by the leaders of his church, and how this experience freed him from religion so he could better follow Jesus. This chapter is a great encouragement to all who have been cast out or condemned by church members and church leaders of former churches.

Travis Klassen shows the truth that Christendom is a hard habit to break. He tried to plant a church with some others that would be different from other churches, but soon found himself in a place full of rules and policies just like any other church. He is now learning to break free again, and is learning to run in the freedom of Jesus Christ.

Following the style of Jesus' Seven Letters to the Churches in Revelation 2–3, Tyson Phillips writes a letter full of pain and sorrow to his former church. They were not there at his times of greatest need, but made sure to point out his every mistake and problem. For these reasons, Tyson has followed Jesus elsewhere.

Tara Pohlkotte brings tears to your eyes as she writes about growing up in a judgmental and critical church and the pain this caused herself and her family. She wants her own children to see Jesus, and her chapter includes a letter she wrote to her children about the Jesus she knows, loves, follows, and serves.

Will Rochow writes about his transition from traditional, institutional church to organic, missional church. He emphasizes the importance and necessity of love as a prerequisite for any expression of church.

Brian Swan was addicted to the powerful and dangerous drug of church attendance and Bible knowledge. He writes about the overwhelming and all-consuming power of this addiction, how he came to recognize it, and what he did to break free and remain clean. He also writes about how he found true community with Christ and with others outside of "church."

A painful church experience is magnified in a digital age where gossip and slander can spread through social networks faster than ever before. Genevieve Thul learned this through personal experience. In her chapter, the pain is present, but is overcome by hope and love. She concludes with several suggestions for people who find themselves attacked and slandered by church people.

CHAPTER 1
HOW SEMINARY HELPED ME LEAVE CHURCH

By Lew Ayotte, Jr.

It was 2003 when I met my future wife. I was a self-proclaimed agnostic and practicing atheist. My future wife was a conservative Christian, of the Southern Baptists persuasion. I liked her, I *really* liked her, but I thought she was an idiot for believing in God. To be honest, my general curiosity as to why people believed this nonsense was one of the reasons I continued talking with her (that and because she is extremely attractive). Our conversations led me to understand my own biases against God and his *followers*. I began to realize that the contradictions and hypocrisies I had witnessed in the people who called themselves Christians should not be applied to what or who God actually is. It was through these epiphanies that God started to work in me and eventually led me to consent to his love.

NEW LIFE

Having been created a new man at the age of 23, I did not share the same theological foundation as my future wife, a preacher's kid, who had been raised in the traditions of the Southern Baptists. Knowing that I needed to catch up, I set out to learn as much as possible about what I was supposed to believe. I dived headlong into the world of Conservative-Bible-Believing-Christianity. I started to attend a small Independent Baptist church down the street from my house, I read theological books, and tried to do anything else I could do to further build my *Foundation of Truth*. Through this, I started to see in myself the potential to become a shepherd of God's flock. At the time, I thought, "pastor" meant "vocational pastor." I saw the pastorate as a paid position, performed by one man leading a group of Christians who met every Sunday morning, evening and sometimes on Wednesdays to hear from God's Word.

As my new bride and I were driving through North Carolina on our honeymoon, I confessed to her that I felt God calling me to become a pastor. She was thrilled to hear this news. We cried, and prayed, and talked about our future as we continued traveling to Maine. After our honeymoon we decided to start our new life together by joining a new church. One of my cousins, a Southern Baptist missionary, mentioned a new Southern Baptist church plant close to us. We decided to visit and soon became members. I learned a lot about the church during my membership: how to order worship services, how to prepare sermons, how to hold business meetings, and how to run discipleship courses. I also met some really great people, people who loved Jesus and wanted to serve him. During this time of learning, I applied to a different college and planned to finish my bachelor's degree at a seminary in North Carolina. I was taking my first steps in following God's calling in my life to become a pastor.

SEMINARY

My wife and I were excited and anxious for this new step in our new lives together. We were ecstatic when I received my acceptance letter and began preparing for our big move to seminary. It was late 2004 when we finally moved to our new home. Thankfully, I secured a job at the seminary, which paid for my tuition, and I eagerly started classes in the spring of 2005.

Having been a Christian for just under two years, I knew I still had much to learn, but I never expected my journey would lead me in a completely different direction. Coming from a background in Technology, I struggled through my first semester. I was not very good at reading and comprehending these materials, even worse at writing about them. But I buckled down, had some great teachers willing to be patient with me, and I studied hard. As is typical with my personality, I found the apologetic classes to be the most interesting. I also spent a lot of time trying to learn Greek and Hebrew. I did quite well.

Around this same time I met a group of men who were probably some of the most influential men that I have ever had in my life. These men taught me something that has changed my life and my theology, forever. These men taught me to ask one simple question, "Why?" Perhaps I am putting it too simplistically. It wasn't just "Why?" It was more than that, it was…

> *Why do we do what we do? Where is it found in the Bible? How do we justify the things that aren't found in the Bible? How do we handle it when the Bible contradicts our positions?*

They taught me to question everything and to pursue God in finding those answers. Of course, this process did not happen overnight, but evolved across my entire seminary experience. The more I learned about traditional Christianity, the more I realized the traditions we practiced were only a few centuries old.

As I became more confident in asking these new questions and learning from my conclusions, I started to share these questions with my fellow students, professors, and with the church—usually to their displeasure. I vividly remember one day in class, we were talking about possible activities to use in a youth group program. I questioned the requirement to have the youth memorize verses of Scripture. Personally, I have a horrible memory but I also mentioned that this requirement could not be found in Scripture. Almost instantly, another classmate shouted to me, "What about Psalm 119, 'I have hidden your word in my heart that I might not sin against you.'" I responded by asking, "Does 'hidden' mean memorized? Was 'your word' referring to the words of Scripture? Are these proclamations prescriptive for us today?" Of course, I was not saying that memorizing Scripture was wrong or evil and I still do not think that, but it is also not a requirement to follow Jesus. Ultimately, I was challenging an important part of this man's faith, something he had held onto as true for a very long time and it disturbed him greatly when someone questioned it.

I also fondly recall a Sunday school class I was teaching. We were talking about the word *church*. I mentioned in passing that it was funny to me that so many groups of Christians put signs in front of their buildings that helped differentiate their beliefs from other groups of Christians. You visit with a Baptist church because they believe and teach Baptist things; you visit with a Lutheran church because they believe and teach Lutheran things. I talked about how we were all the church together, we all belonged to Christ and we should welcome any other Christ-follower into our group. Some of the people started to talk about what could go on the sign, if not, "Baptist Church of *Somewhere*." A nice lady thought long and hard about this and asked, "Could we put 'Church of Christ' on the sign?" and immediately a man in the back proclaimed, "There is no way we are putting *Church of Christ* on our sign! Church of Christ is a completely different denomination!" I think he failed to see the point I was trying to make.

Through my time at the seminary, I continued to bring up alternative views in my Sunday school classes. When given the opportunity, I preached sermons trying to spark people to question their beliefs and practices. I asked similar questions in my seminary classes, hoping that my fellow classmates would begin to seek out the answers. I spoke with people privately and encouraged them to ask similar questions about why they believed what they believed. Few responded positively.

Perhaps it was my approach or how I was presenting my ideas. Maybe I was too young or I made people uncomfortable. Ultimately, they were happy with the status quo; they did not want to upset Eve's apple cart. They often agreed with me to my face, but when it came down to action, they could not pull themselves away from the modern Christian experience to which they were accustomed. By the end of my experience as a student at seminary, I had come to wildly different conclusions about the church than what I expect my professors would have thought kosher. Though I still believe to this day that God has called me to be a pastor and teacher to His church, I also believe it is in an extremely different capacity than the *vocational pastor* model to which I had originally been introduced.

A BETTER WAY

Today a pastor earns his living by preaching sermons, visiting the sick, teaching Wednesday night Bible studies, and coordinating business meetings. A layperson earns their peace of mind by paying the pastor to work on their behalf. Both of these people play an integral part in the economy of the modern church. When I started to question this economy, I realized that I was moving away from these groups of people. As much as I wanted to stay, to be a change, to help them see that there was a better way, I could not do any good. I began to feel more and more like staying in the system only encouraged the system to grow and people like me would continue to be shoved to the side and ignored.

Moving to Georgia was the perfect opportunity for my wife and I to leave the church. Once we had settled into our new home we tried and visited a few traditional churches, we really wanted to experience Christian fellowship, but we discovered quickly that nothing had changed. A few people would greet us, many would run around the traditional 60-second handshake lap, then we would sit quietly to listen to the pastor speak for 30 minutes and once it was over we would go home and continue our normal lives—just like everyone else. This was not fellowship; this was not encouraging each other to love and good works I read about in Hebrews 10:24. To us this was pointless, and eventually we simply stopped trying.

Ultimately, this story is about how and why we left the church. Though we have left the church in one sense, in another we have not left the church. I believe there is a better way. I believe this better way is described in Scripture. I believe we fear following Scripture, because it is so liberating. Freedom is scary. What if everyone felt free to speak? What if someone teaches, or says something wrong? What if we do not agree with another's interpretations? What if the children are too loud?

What if life happens when we gather together?

There is a better way to *do church*. Communing together, learning from one another, experiencing life with one another, teaching, praying, working, giving, playing ... and living. When we can learn to do these things together, I truly believe we will thrive and fulfill the calling that God has already placed in all of our hearts.

Yes, I have left the church, but more importantly, as we journey together with Jesus I continue to find the church.

CHAPTER 2
MY JOURNEY OUT OF CHURCH

By Carey Crawford

I was brought up in a solid, stable home with parents who loved me and cared deeply about my spiritual well being. My early spiritual formation took place in a small town country church where my whole family attended each Sunday and Wednesday. The adage "We were there every time the doors were open" was true for us, not only because we believed it was our duty to faithfully attend, but also because my dad was the Minister of Music, and later my mom was the church custodian. So we were the ones who actually opened the doors for each activity and service. Although many years have passed since then, my mother and two brothers along with their families still are involved at my home church. My brothers are both in leadership roles there.

Early on, the pastor took an interest in me and provided opportunities to be involved in areas of ministry. Even as a teenager, I taught a class of younger teens on Sunday evenings. God used my early experiences in this church to bring me to faith in Him, give me a strong foundation in the faith, and awaken a desire to be used by God in ministry. That desire followed me into my college years.

EARLY MINISTRY

While studying for a business degree at the University of Mississippi, I reached a point of dissatisfaction with the direction of my life. My wife and I had married after our first semester, and she sensed the uncertainty in my soul. One day she asked, "Do you think God is calling you to preach?" I said no, but I wasn't sure of my answer. I spoke with the pastor in our church near campus. I shared that I sensed God might be calling me into ministry. He simply said, "I know." It was like everything fell into place. My confusion and dissatisfaction evaporated. I knew what I was supposed to do. I had never been so certain of anything in my life.

My seminary training began right after graduation from college. I was hungry and eager to become equipped to serve God in full-time vocational ministry. During seminary I was given several opportunities to begin utilizing my gifts and putting my newly acquired skills and knowledge into practice. I taught Sunday school, served as a youth chaperone, and preached every chance I got. Churches without pastors or with pastors on vacation would call me to fill the pulpit. Those were great years, during which time God shaped my style of teaching, preaching, and leadership.

PROFESSIONAL MINISTRY YEARS

For quite a while I intentionally turned down opportunities to become a candidate at churches seeking a pastor, because I sensed I was not ready for full-time pastoral ministry. But the day finally came in 1995 after I had served a stint as an Associate State Missionary in Mississippi for two years. A church in Louisiana called me, and I felt a peace from God about agreeing to go and interview with them. We wound up going to that little church of less than fifty members on the outskirts of West Monroe, Louisiana. We pastored those dear people for eight and a half years.

By 2003 I had a growing realization that I had taken this church as far as they would go with me. A church in Dallas, TX called and wanted to interview me. I agreed, and after a series of interviews and preaching in their services, they called me to serve as their pastor. We moved to Dallas in October 2003 and served in that church for just over seven years. It was while we were in this church that God began reshaping my basic philosophy about how churches operate and do ministry. My focus began to shift from working to grow my church to asking questions about how we could grow the kingdom of God.

About this same time, it began to dawn on me that I had come to a church that was in a downhill slide toward its grave. Only four years before I arrived, the church had gone through a devastating split. As I began to research the numbers, it became apparent the church never recovered from this split. All of the ministry energy of the church went toward keeping the church on life support. It seemed that our main goal was to keep the doors open for the saints. I saw that the mission of the church was not so much on bringing the love of God to people outside of Christ, but how we could get more people through the doors and into the pews on Sunday. In my spirit I knew something was not right about how we were doing church.

At a meeting of our Budget and Finance Committee, I pointed out how much of the church's income went toward maintaining the building. I posed the question, "What if we had no building to worry about? How much more real ministry could be done with those funds if we didn't have to pay for insurance, repairs, lawn care, and light bulbs?" The question sparked some conversation that ultimately led to a vision to sell the building and relaunch as a new church entirely. We found a buyer for the property two weeks after putting it on the market, and in April 2010 we had our final service there. The next week, those who planned to go with the new church began meeting in a school cafeteria.

TRANSFORMING CHURCH

Shortly after we launched in this new direction for the church, I became convicted that we were about to head down the same road we had just exited. We were planning energetic worship services, creative childcare, and engaging, relevant sermon series. I realized that church is not to be centered on the Sunday event, but on the day-in, day-out routine of regular life. It is there that God works! We had always said to people, "Come to church and see what God will do!" My growing conviction was that we had to switch our expectations to "Watch what God is doing in your workplace, your school, and your neighborhood, and get involved there. Then let's gather on Sunday to celebrate what God has done." That shift in thinking was revolutionary for me!

I found others who were thinking in the same direction. I began reading about missional/incarnational living, and it clicked. The idea of *being* the church over *doing* church resonated with me. I began to see that how we were doing church was actually hindering the mission of God in our lives and in our community. So I began reexamining the Scriptures through a fresh set of eyes to try to learn what the church was supposed to be. I came to realize that the church could be expressed in a myriad of ways, that there was no holy cookie-cutter approach that everyone must use. For me, the most essential definition of the church came to be, "People in Relationship on Mission."

Another part of my transformation was how the "call to ministry" is understood. In my tradition, that phrase is reserved for preachers, missionaries, and those who would serve as ministers on church staff. God showed me that every believer is called into ministry, because we are first called into relationship with Jesus. It is out of that relationship that our ministry call is uniquely expressed. For some the expression of their ministry may be working at Starbucks, being a teacher in the local middle school, or driving a forklift in a grocery warehouse. For others, it may be serving as a pastor or volunteering for community events. The point is that the call is on every believer, and you are most satisfied when you are expressing that call in the context of a vibrant personal relationship with Jesus Christ. It's not the ministry activity itself, or the amount of ministry activity that is the priority: It's the relationship with Jesus that is the priority. Another thing I have discovered is that the expression of the call on my life will change over the years. It used to be that if you were called to be a pastor, that's the role you would fill the rest of your life. It is liberating to know that roles can change, because I now see that God is at work in all of life. I am free to go anywhere and be anything for Christ. There is no more division between sacred and secular or clergy and laity. My calling has never been so rewarding. I now focus on developing missional communities while encouraging and training others in the incarnational lifestyle.

My struggle and misgivings were never about the church itself, but about the structures and systems constructed around the church that needed to be administrated and maintained so that ministry could happen. Along the way, the church began to believe that if we did not have certain things, such as a building, staff, a budget, and programs, we were not a real church. Ministry was professionalized to such a degree that "regular Christians" (the laypeople) felt they were not qualified to do it.

I am no longer satisfied with church as usual. To go back into leading a church under the incorporation guidelines would kill my spirit. I have made the choice, not to abandon the church, but to lead the church back into the living organism it was meant to be.

CHAPTER 3
MY ROAD TO LEAVING CHURCH

By Michael Donahoe

I grew up in a Christian family and was one of the kids who never got in trouble. I didn't smoke, didn't drink, didn't cuss, and was always in church whenever the doors were open. I believed that attending church was one primary way of showing that I was different than the world. I believed that God was pleased by my actions, my attitude, and how much I attended church. I was such a good Christian; I actually began to think I might be one of God's favorites.

In talking with people, I was always interested to find out where they went to church. If they went to the same type of church as I did, I felt they were all right. If they attended a different kind of church—or no church at all—I figured there was something wrong with them. I also made sure to invite my unsaved friends to church rather than talk to them about what Christ did for me. I felt it was my job to invite people to church; it was the church's job to evangelize those I brought. I thought that if I got them to church, the pastor would take care of everything else.

EIGHT STEPS AWAY FROM CHURCH

In the last few years I've had a groaning deep inside about the modern-day church. There hasn't been one major thing that happened to me, but in an ongoing, step-by-step process, I have come to view church in a whole new way.

First, I began to question denominations. I wondered why there were so many different groups of people and why those groups couldn't seem to get along with people of a different denomination. Though Jesus called us to show love for one another (John 13:35), it seems like people from different denominations prefer to fight and argue with others because of differences in church practices and biblical understanding. Where are the unity and the love?

Second, I wondered why churches spend so much money on material things rather than on the mission of Jesus. Churches of all shapes and sizes spend money on bigger buildings, a nicer car for the pastor, newer choir robes, and other expenses churches seem to require. While most churches do give to various missions and ministries, it seems a very small percentage of the total giving actually goes to ministries that help others in tangible ways.

Third, it always bothered me that we Christians dress up and act differently on Sunday. We put on our Sunday best not just in what we wear, but also in how we behave. What is it about church that does not allow us to be who we truly are? Though people claimed that the church was God's house, the Bible says that God's house is within us.

Fourth, the church seemed focused on Old Covenant living. Many of the events and teachings of the church centered on keeping the Old Covenant law. Yet we are saved by grace through faith and nothing we do or fail to do makes a difference in our salvation. We can't make God more pleased with us by doing things and we can't make him mad at us for not doing something. Focusing on the law leads to Pharisaical living.

Fifth, a big aggravation was how people looked up to the pastor and the leaders of the church. It seemed like they were almost on a different level than the rest of the congregation. This tendency to put the pastor on a pedestal had the by-product of expecting the pastor to do all the work. People assume the pastor is paid to do the work of the ministry so they can sit and enjoy the service.

Sixth, I became frustrated when worship leaders told me how to worship, when to raise my hands, when to clap, when to pray, when to say "Amen," when to sit, and when to stand. If I did not respond as directed, I was made to feel guilty, as if I was not actually worshipping God. Shouldn't worship come from genuine love for God and not because someone is trying to pump it up to make the worship team look good?

Seventh, I was always told that I had to be in church to get good fellowship. But good fellowship in church seems to consist of sitting in church for an hour every week, looking at the back of the head of the person in front of me. I've wondered how this can be good Christian fellowship when I haven't talked to anyone during the entire service. While Christians do need to continue in fellowship with other believers, and we must not forsake the assembling of ourselves together (Heb 10:25), the Bible does not say anywhere that this fellowship has to be in a building on a certain day. Christians can fellowship anytime, anywhere.

Finally, there is tithing. What can I say? Tithing is an Old Covenant law and is no longer a requirement for living in grace. We give out of love and according to how we feel God is leading us, in response to needs that God brings to our attention. I think the clergy pushes tithing only because they need a salary, the church mortgage has to be paid, and expenses need to be met.

LEAVING CHURCH TO BE THE CHURCH

I struggled with these feelings about church for a long time, and wondered what was going on with me. Was something wrong with my fellowship with God? Was I getting tired of church and Christianity after all this time?

I finally came to the conclusion that going to church is not the answer. There is certainly more to church than sitting in a building and letting someone else tell me what God was saying. God said that we, his people, are the temples of the Holy Spirit. God lives in us, not in a building. He says we are all sheep and he is the Shepherd, not the person we call pastor that gets up each week and talks about what they think the Bible says.

So I have pretty much stopped attending church. I do think that church, or what I now like to call a religious meeting place, is a good place for Christian people to get together socially, but it is not God's house and it is not the church.

I still battle with my decision to leave the church. I have so many friends that are part of the organized church and they don't understand my feelings. I often feel as if I am on my own, and it makes me feel like it would be easier to keep my mouth shut and keep on attending services like normal. But returning to church in this way would just be to please men and would not be a result of trying to follow the leading of the Spirit. I am fortunate to have my wife and a couple of guys I meet with every other week who have the same feelings.

I now know in my mind that I have not truly left church because I am a part of the church, which is not a building we enter, but is the people of God who are saved by grace. I know that fellowship with other believers can take place anywhere and anytime. I am part of the church every day no matter where I am, or what I am doing.

CHAPTER 4
AN EPICAL ECCLESIASTICAL ADVENTURE

By Glenn Hager

My relationship with the organized church has run the entire spectrum of involvement. I have been a heavily vested insider, a stalker who wanted to crash the party with my reforms, and an outsider who finds what goes on there irrelevant to my life.

I did a twenty-year plus stint as a senior pastor of three different churches. Having gone to a very fundamentalist Bible college, I was a conservative's conservative.

PLANTING A LOVING CHURCH

My first church was a start-up begun by some people unhappy with the stodgy First Baptist Church in town. Unfortunately, it was the third Southern Baptist church in the small community. One was stodgy, one was charismatic, and ours was loving and geared toward the down-and-outers in town.

The church grew as we reached out to the folks from "the other side of the tracks." Actually, we lived on "the other side of the tracks." Our neighbors were friendly drug dealers whose children ran amuck throughout the neighborhood until after dark. So our church built a playground for their kids on an empty lot across the street from our duplex.

One of our neighbors died of AIDS, acquired through drug use and her family asked me to have her funeral. This was the early 80s, when AIDS was new and very scary.

Eventually, I grew tired of the smallness and limited growth potential with the fledgling church and began to look for greener pastures.

THE COUNTRY CITY CHURCH

The second church was a pleasant place. They had a beautiful building in a good location in a comfortable sized city. The people were friendly and they loved having a young pastor with a young family who preached a passionate sermon. It was a country, good-ole-boy church that happened to be located in the city. I was well connected within the community and well loved by the congregants. I could have retired a happy man, except George Barna messed everything up for me.

I had begun to wonder why church was not working and why it didn't look anything like the church in Acts 2. Barna confirmed my worst suspicions; the church was stuck in the fifties. This church was really stuck in the fifties, with their love of Southern country Gospel quartets and potluck suppers.

I still remember the church board chairman coming to my office to warn me of a serious issue in which my leadership was causing a stir within the congregation. I had moved the offering to end of the service and people simply did not care for that at all. That was, unfortunately, a pretty good indicator of the depth of the vision of the church. That type of incident, which indicated that my congregants and I held a vastly different set of values, was very demoralizing to me. At those times, I would ask myself, "What have I done moving my family to this community to minister to a congregation that fights such small, insignificant changes?"

All they wanted was someone to preach, visit the shut-ins, pat them on the back, and bury them. But this was not me, especially with my growing inner unrest about what church had become. So, I looked for a church where the leadership took their role more seriously.

THE SUBURBAN CHURCH

Once again, I dragged my family across the Midwest, this time winding up in a large, aging Chicago suburb. This ten-year stint was like a whitewater raft ride in which you eventually crash against the rocks, are thrown from the raft, wash up on the shore, and are left for dead.

The church had been living with the stress of being divided between old fundamentalists and new evangelicals for a long time. They were totally paralyzed. When I arrived on the scene they were weary of plans to find a new mutually agreed upon direction.

Eventually, I declared our mission to be the Great Commission and stated we will evaluate everything in light of that. This show of determination united the two factions in becoming very uncomfortable with my leadership. Through a long and painful process, they all eventually left the church.

All that remained was a tiny group of people who had joined since I had arrived, along with those who never got involved in the fray. We felt a new freedom, fixed up our old building, rewrote the church constitution, drastically changed our worship style, and reworked all of our ministries. We warmed everything up and brought our approach up to current times. Our finances suffered greatly, but another church in the area amazingly supplemented my salary for a couple of years.

We went from organ to band, drawing a bushel of musicians and transitioned into one of the most rockin' churches anywhere. We scrapped every program except worship and small groups. Spontaneous ministry was happening like crazy. I was delighted! We converted to a seeker styled Sunday service with a down and dirty approach, which attracted the down-and-outers we sought to reach.

Eventually, we felt the church needed to move locations, since we were a little Anglo island in our neighborhood. In fact, we hosted a Hispanic congregation for years and they were booming.

We moved to the more affluent suburbs, where we rented office space and a movie theater, and classed up our act to appeal to yuppies. This failed miserably. We were already small and lost some people in the move. Now we were asking these down-and-outers to be a part of a labor-intensive church-in-a-box operation, for which they did not have the energy or time. Yet there was a much more devastating issue brewing.

A seminary professor and author who apparently loved me and couldn't shower me with enough accolades rather suddenly got his nose bent out of shape over the move. He stirred up his son, our worship leader, who staged a coupe right about the time of our relocation. As a result, we lost even more people and could not sustain the costs of the new location.

The church was now so small, that we retreated to my family room for a few months. Eventually, feeling like we were a precious little group of needy people, but not the core of a new church, we disbanded, giving all the money from selling the building and all our equipment to a new, but struggling church in our area.

THE DAY OF DARKNESS

It's been over ten years now, but there is a moment of darkness in this third church that is still etched in my soul. It was a snowy February Sunday near my birthday and it was more than obvious that some relationships were very tense and it was also painfully obvious that we could no longer continue meeting in the theater. But this was my dream. I had paid for it with blood, sweat, and tears, and many years of my life. And now, my dream had turned into a nightmare and I wanted out!

The worst part of watching my dream dissolve was not all of the legalities involved in closing a church, moving all of my books and mementos accumulated over two decades from my office to my home, trying to find a way to explain all this to people, and dealing with the inevitable loss of relationships. The very worst thing for me was trying to figure out who I was.

My relationship with the church was always a love/hate relationship. I loved being the pastor, the preacher, the counselor, the leader, and the go-to-guy. It fed my ego and fit my inner identity. Yet, I never liked the more formal responsibilities like weddings and funerals. I didn't like the crazy scope of expectations that congregants tried to force upon me. I really hated the over possessiveness of church members and their blatant disregard for those outside the fellowship. I was always annoyed by their being out-of-step with the times and the culture, which I took as part of their self-obsessed ways. Yet, I was very much a churchman and I still am very much a pastor at heart.

THE STALKER YEARS

The next eight years of my life were my stalker years. I loved the church, but it had issues, so I tried to help. The first few years I tried to find a new pastor gig. I was an independent with no denominational affiliation, so I was on my own. But closing a church looks bad on your resume. On top of that, I was confined to the area because my wife had a good job that we could not afford to leave. Even my pastor friends acted like I had died and my circle of relationships had fractured along with the closing of the church. I was alone.

I had a few interviews but soon found that churches were looking for a "Brother Bud" or a "Superstar" type of pastor and I had no aspirations of becoming either.

We attended three different established churches and two house churches over the next eight years. One was a church that my old church blessed with tens of thousands of dollars in money and equipment. Their senior pastor was a gifted preacher and musician, but his church board of friends and relatives wanted to keep the pastor cult mentality intact and made it very clear that the only place for me was in the pew.

Another church was a suburban start-up with a delightful, young senior pastor. I helped them with a focus group evaluation of their welcoming ministry and then headed up that ministry, but we weren't too into the whole suburban scene.

The third was a larger, trendy church. I also ran their welcoming ministry and coordinated a huge community display of kindness in which we gave away two truckloads of food, set up a social service expo, and sponsored other community projects. They were struggling financially and decided to decrease their involvement in their community outreach to the poor, rather than cut building or program expenses. It seemed hypocritical to me.

For a while, we had a regular group at our home with unchurched young adults asking awesome questions. I loved it, but it wasn't something with much of a lifespan, since some of these kids where still looking for the next party. We attended a couple of other house churches that eventually died, but didn't feel very connected with them either.

As a stalker, I encountered varying levels of receptiveness from being totally shut out to being humored for a while. I finally realized I was like a bird, one that had been freed from his cage, and strangely kept trying to break back in. I was trying to change the church by dealing with people who had too much vested interest in church and too much at risk.

During this time, I experienced various degrees of unemployment. I have been unemployed, underemployed, and mis-employed for ten years. During that time, I have washed windows, sold cars, had my own window cleaning and painting company, and worked as an account manager for a high tech company. I hated each of those jobs; with the exception of the times my son would help me on painting jobs.

For a long, long time, I was lonely and lost, not being able to get a handle on my identity or figure out how to earn an income. During this time my two best friends died, one of cancer and one in a car accident. There have been times that I stared up at the night sky and asked God what he was doing. But I believe that these experiences are part of the process by which God shapes me to better empathize with those who also feel there is no place for them in church.

Like many others in the world, I am an outsider. I have not attended a church service for over two years. I don't care about church politics, church trends, or when a church leader says something stupid. Now, it seems like a game to me, a rather foolish one.

The whole idea of a weekly pep rally to whip people into frenzy or to get them feeling guilty seems unnatural. I don't like the concept of using costly real estate exclusively for insider purposes. I don't like the concept of paying a pastor who does traditional pastor things. I don't like the idea of churches trying to be cool. I do not like the idea of a programmed approach to ministry. I really do not like the self-serving nature of the majority of what most churches do. However, I don't mind that people are into it, because most of them are sincere, good-hearted people.

THE CHURCH OF THE FUTURE

I am undecided about the church of the future. I believe one approach will be small groups of friends who informally discuss life and what it means to follow Jesus. For established churches, there is a wonderful opportunity to become community centers that focus on tangible ways of displaying Christ's love to the people of their community.

I am a little lonely in my present state, but don't like the concept of trying to organize something. That needs to be an agreement between friends. When we organize something there is a keeper of the vision and eventually, someone has a different vision and then it starts to get ugly.

I am a different person; more open to divergent ideas, more into the moment, and more relational. I think I am a somewhat nicer human being since I have left the pastorate and the organized church behind. My son jokingly told some friends that I am pretty much the same, except I have ditched the suit and now listen to Metallica and drink beer.

Nothing makes more sense to me than trying to live a fully integrated life in which you witness God at work everywhere and not just in the confines of an organization or a building. At last, I am beginning to get comfortable with that idea.

CHAPTER 5
JANETTE'S CHURCH CRISIS

By Wayne W. Hobson

A friend who belonged to church with an abusive pastor told the following story to me. She still struggles with her relationship with God due to the abusive nature of her spiritual leader and church. Through the hearing of this story, I, a minister myself, aspire to be a dedicated servant of Jesus Christ and pray that I never become the spiritual tyrant that this pastor was. Names and minor details have been altered to protect the individuals in the story.

JANETTE'S STORY

Janette's story is indeed a harrowing one. She had moved from Atlanta to Philadelphia with her two young sons, ages two and five. Janette had been a Jehovah's Witness (part of her family's background) in Atlanta, but became disillusioned with the group's critical judgment of her two pregnancies outside of wedlock. She left the Witnesses shortly before moving to Philly and decided that a more traditional church setting might prove to be spiritually enriching. Unfortunately for her, the church that she became involved with was neither traditional nor enriching. At the recommendation of a friend, Janette joined a fellowship named Independent Christ Church (ICC). Janette was searching for a pastor that could teach her about who God really was and her friend assured her that the "Apostle," the pastor of ICC, was the person Janette needed to see. With little money and even fewer resources since her move (they lived in a homeless shelter at the time), Janette hoped that ICC was the answer.

She met with the "Apostle," who told her that ICC was a non-denominational Charismatic "Deliverance Ministry" that felt called to revitalize young people such as herself. He arranged for her and her sons to have somewhere to stay and she became a faithful member — or so she thought. The Apostle and his wife ran the church, attempting to control many aspects of their followers' lives. The Apostle demanded that the young men in the church should imitate him, dressing as he did (in expensive suits), the women were to imitate his wife, and no one of the singles were to date anyone or be involved in relationships. Church services were long, with excessive praise and worship that lasted for 5-6 hours or more. These would often last through the night, well into the early morning, which made it difficult for those who had to go to work the next day. The Apostle insisted that Janette and her sons attend each service — after all, she was indebted to him and the church for helping her in her time of need.

WHAT'S WRONG WITH THIS PICTURE?

Janette began to realize that something was really wrong with this "church" when the Apostle yelled at her two year old son for making noise during one of his long tirade-like sermons. The boy was simply engaged in childhood play, yet the Apostle lashed out at him and Janette. The boy was unaware that he was "disturbing the service" and continued to play. The Apostle grabbed the boy and shook him, yelling that the child had an evil spirit of rebellion in him. The Apostle demanded that the "evil spirit" come out. The child was frightened and began crying. Janette grabbed her son and sat him down next to her. She could not understand what just happened. She was totally confused now. Did she do something wrong? Did her son? Was the Apostle wrong? She was at a loss for words. The Apostle later apologized and told her that God had dealt with him for the way he treated her son. Still, she couldn't leave the church at this point — she and her sons needed a place to live and she felt that she owed ICC for helping her.

She began to notice other strange things in the church services. He had said that he was the church members' spiritual father and insisted on being referred to as "Dad." On occasions when people disagreed with any of the Apostle's actions, they were singled out, openly rebuked, and told that they had "evil spirits." He gave names to these so-called demons, like "I hate father spirit" or "a disobedient spirit." The Apostle made a spectacle of Janette in a few services when he threw her and her sons out (told them to leave) simply because they made facial expressions during the Apostle's sermon. These types of experiences traumatized her and her family. Both Janette and her sons began to have seizures after this point. Though it cannot be conclusively said that the seizures were definitively caused by their involvement in ICC, neither Janette nor her sons had experienced any seizure activity before joining the church.

On a number of occasions during church services, some women's undergarment and body parts (including Janette's) were exposed while they were supposedly "slain in the Spirit" (a phenomenon in which people seem to faint due to what is believed to be a moving of the Holy Spirit). When church members would attempt to cover the exposed women, the Apostle would stop them from doing so, claiming that "The power of the anointing was too strong."

The Apostle and his wife lived lavishly at the expense of the church membership, which were predominately young people, who like Janette, were financially disadvantaged. Yet the Apostle insisted that the church owed him and his wife all-expense paid vacations and the financial support for the lifestyle they were accustomed to. Men in the church would chauffer the Apostle around town and would do menial tasks like take out his trash or pick up his dry cleaning. Meanwhile, the church leaders subjected Janette and the other young women to close scrutiny. If she or anyone else said anything against the Apostle, those who were eavesdropping immediately reported the conversation to him.

THE STRAW THAT BROKE THE CAMEL'S BACK

Janette and her sons had been at ICC for about seven years now and her oldest son, now 12, had tried to fit in with the church's "ideology." He loved cars and had a few driving lessons from a couple of men in the church. A church staff member was assigned to park the Apostle's car during a service one day. The keys were left in the car and Janette's son asked the staff member if he could park the vehicle. The man jokingly told the boy yes, but the boy jumped in the car and pulled off before the staff knew it, and crashed the Apostle's car into a store next to the church. The boy escaped any serious injury, but the vehicle suffered moderate damage to the front bumper, hood, and engine.

The Apostle was furious. The male staff person lied about the incident, claiming that he never gave Janette's son permission to park the car. As a result, the Apostle instructed the "men" in the church to severely punish the 12 year old. He was punched by the group of men repeated on various parts of his body. The boy suffered bruises and minor cuts. Janette had seen enough! She immediately left the church after finding out what happened. Though the police were notified of the incident, Janette does not know what became of the situation. She moved back to Atlanta shortly after that. To this day, she and her sons still experience seizures from time to time. And sadly, to this day, she has never joined or set foot in a church again.

CHAPTER 6
HOW PROFESSOR P. J. GOMES HELPED ME QUESTION EVANGELICALISM

By Judith Huang

By the second semester of my Harvard College career, I was already (in my own mind) a cool cat when it came to the wily ruses to get into good sections of my classes. This is how I did it: I signed up for Reverend Gomes' Christian Bible and its Interpreters, but sneakily didn't enter my name for the section lotteries. Instead, I simply turned up at Professor Gomes' Wednesday section, and insinuated myself as a member. It was in an underground room in Memorial Church—the only class I took my four years in that building. The room was appropriately lined with dark wood, crimson wallpaper, and a particularly obnoxiously loud and handsome grandfather clock. Professor Gomes sat in the middle of a long table like Jesus in Da Vinci's "The Last Supper."

"Hoom!" was the first sound he made when it turned out the class list didn't quite tally with the one he had been given. Sitting in the middle of the table was a beautiful ledger with cream paper and a bulbous fountain pen. We were all supposed to write our names in it for attendance at the start of class. My fifteen compatriots and I looked uneasily at one another, until one of the braver ones took up the pen, a thing of silver and marble, and proceeded to scratch his name awkwardly in the ledger. When the book got to me, I felt like a chicken scratching her name in the Book of Life, but fortunately the six names above mine bore the same marks of strenuous effort. We introduced ourselves sharing our reasons for taking the class. Two of her previous siblings had taken it. Her parents were nervous now that she was taking it. Gomes chuckled appreciatively.

"Ah, so you, too, are here to lose your faith!"

I was slightly alarmed. I had been warned about this sort of thing — my church was the sort where concerned housewives pulled you aside to tell you not to study literature at university, or preferably not to go to university at all, "in case you lose your faith." It was a good thing that the serious state of degeneration of mainline Protestantism in the Northeast had yet to reach the ears of tropical Singaporeans half a world away. At the same time, I felt a kind of illicit thrill, the nerd's equivalent of taking the first puff of a cigarette behind school. Perhaps I *would* be corrupted! The chorus of R.E.M.'s "Losing my Religion" rang in my head. My church back home thought R.E.M. (and Harry Potter, and James Bond) was Satanic. I felt myself at the precipice of a very long and slippery slope.

GOD CHURCH BIBLE

I enjoyed the class immensely. I was taking it for fun. I read with literary interest about Christian typology. I was shocked and delighted to learn Augustine had warned against literalism centuries before my country had even been founded.

Professor Gomes' lectures were always an event. The man was a self-conscious fulfilment of everything any of us had dreamed a Harvard professor would be. I am pretty sure he did it on purpose. He would stride into Harvard Hall, walking stick in hand, a vision of tweed and pocket-squares and watch-chains, and carelessly (but theatrically) toss his fedora in a way that made it land precisely on the window ledge of the first window on the right, alarming students sitting on the next one. Job well done, he would write the three words "GOD CHURCH BIBLE" on the board, and launch into his subject with that booming voice of his.

To say it challenged my evangelical, Calvinist, dispensationalist worldview is an understatement. By the end of the class, I was shaken and stirred. Major theologians jostled for space in my head. I didn't know what to do about the final project. I talked to him about it, and in his infinite kindness and understanding, he assigned me Karl Barth.

DINNER WITH GOMES

One of the most glorious experiences I had at Harvard was the dinner Professor Gomes threw to conclude the class. It was in the wonderful rose-red Pusey room, on the second floor of Memorial church—another room outfitted to his instruction. We were ushered into the room, seated at great round tables, and when Gomes rose to give a toast, instructed us to read the text that was inscribed (by his instruction) along the top of the walls of that room. Squinting, we read "Here is Wisdom; here is the Royal Law; here are the Lively Oracles of God."

"To the Lively Oracles of God!" he said, lifting his glass with glee. "And let that cry shake the very stones!" I am certain he has left more than just these little clues, scattered around and about the campus, anchoring Harvard to its true origins, to its moral core.

Him being a proud eschewer of email, I thought I would never be able to contact him again when the course completed, but I was wrong. I was to have several more encounters before I graduated. Whether it was the steward of the Signet Society ("We do not do, we *are*."), complaining about budgeting for his refurbishment of the dining rooms ("Professor Gomes has exquisite, but expensive, taste!"), to finding myself on the editorial board of the *Harvard Ichthus* (a journal of Christian thought) which he lent the moral support of his name on the masthead, Gomes permeated the atmosphere of Harvard.

This, too, was a case in point in how fancy dinners can have stellar uses. In my junior year, I saw a tiny ad in the Harvard Gazette for a "Vocations Dinner" at Sparks' House, where he held his weekly teas. As a Myers-Briggs INFJ obsessed with the word "vocation" and feeling particularly directionless at the time, I knew I had to sign up. It was all the pomp you could imagine, with very silent butlers and clinking silver and every imaginable sort of cheese. When Professor Gomes stood up to clink his glass to welcome those who were interested in making a career out of ministry, he set to dispelling the myth that it would necessarily impoverish us. "Some of us, as you can see, do quite well for ourselves," he said, waving airily at the cheese platters.

There were seating cards at this dinner, and I was seated next to Samir Paul, the dashing young man who had just received the mission to revive the readership and circulation of *The Ichthus*. From there on, *The Ichthus* became the consuming passion of my Harvard life, and I had Gomes to thank for it.

HARVARD STYLE

The thing about Professor Gomes was that he had style. Sometimes this was infuriating, and some people held it against him. Perhaps from years of being in charge of fiercely ecumenical Memorial Church, he had honed the art of the evasive witticism. "Do you believe in God?" "Well, God believes in *you*." "Do you believe in the Trinity?" "Well, it *is* traditional." Always pithy, sometimes maddening, he could seem two-dimensional, or, more accurately, opaque.

He clearly enjoyed pomp and ceremony, and *believed* in them in a nearly sacramental way. He enjoyed recounting dinners with English Catholic aristocrats ("Who always managed to keep their heads.") and holding tasteful dinners redolent of Old Harvard. In his way, he was one of the keepers of Old Harvard, simultaneously incongruous and more Harvardy than anything else. (To place it in context, most of Harvard for me consisted of wearing a hoodie and typing out papers while procrastinating on Facebook.) My more evangelical friends liked to dislike him for his equivocation, and those who were suspicious of WASP-iness disliked him for his airs and graces. I must admit I held some of the same reservations, as I distrusted my own enjoyment of the pomp and privilege that was being at Harvard.

But it all melted away in an unexpected place—in the office of poetry critic Helen Vendler. She told me a story about Professor Gomes, which I was able to relate to a friend. Just before I graduated, I was talking to a friend who was struggling deeply with his sexuality and his religion. Like me, he had been brought up evangelical, but the sort of thing he had grown up believing cut him more deeply and closely than I could imagine, for he was just coming to terms with being gay, a thing his family hoped would be merely temporary. He was one of my friends who liked to make Professor Gomes and Unitarian jokes.

"Do you want to hear a touching story about Professor Gomes?" I asked him.

"No, I don't want to hear a touching story about Professor Gomes."

I went ahead anyway. "Helen Vendler told me that, in the nineties, during the AIDS epidemic, there was a lot of demonstrating for and against homosexuality in the college. And there was this one undergrad who had holed himself up in his room when he had found out he tested positive. He refused to come out for weeks and weeks. His friends brought him food, but it would just lie outside the room, and they were all afraid he would commit suicide. Months went by. Then, the only person who managed to reach him and coax him out was Professor Gomes, because he sat outside his door and waited until he did."

My friend was silent for a moment.

"Yes, that was a touching story. I'm touched."

And really, that's what it was. It wasn't that, in an act of extraordinary bravery, Professor Gomes had stood on the steps of Memorial church in the face of an angry mob and come out as gay, and a Christian. It wasn't that he was one of only two black men on the faculty when he first started at Harvard. It wasn't that he knew every theologian and American historical movement in Christianity inside out. It was that he cared deeply and sacrificially for that one boy. After hearing that story, I knew that this man knew God. Although I don't see myself returning to my old church, I think I am a better Christian for it.

Professor Gomes complicated my faith — made it less lazy, more honest, and more complex — but he didn't make me lose it.

GRADUATION

In the spring of 2010, up the steps of Memorial church, the soon-to-be-graduates entered boisterously two by two. Professor Gomes, his red cloak billowing behind him, stood with both hands held out, round-framed glasses tilted slightly up over deep-set eyes, booming his congratulations to each undergrad who passed by. I reached out to grasp his hand and thank him. "Did you know that *The Ichthus* now blogs every day?" I told him.

"I am very pleased to hear that, my dear. Very pleased," he boomed. "I am very glad, for I was an early investor." All eyebrows and eyelids, he gives me a wink.

Later, during the graduation service, one of my atheist friends whispered, "This is so Old Harvard! It's so… anachronistic that we have go to church to get blessed before we graduate. By a Professor of Christian Morals."

"Yeah…"

"But you know, it's sort of like, if there wasn't such a thing, you'd feel kind of cheated, somehow. Like you aren't really graduating from Harvard." I knew Professor Gomes would have liked to hear that.

During the processional, I call out to him as he passed by. "Professor Gomes! I seek your blessing!"

"You have it!" he said, flourishing his wand and tapping me with it. And I still feel blessed.

CHAPTER 7
A HERETIC AMONG US

By Mike Keffer

I grew up in extreme poverty as a child and because I was smart and grew up in the country, I threw myself into my schoolwork and athletics to escape my home life. I earned straight A's and lettered in football and basketball yet these achievements meant nothing to my mom and dad who never attended any sporting event nor did they recognize my academic efforts. However, when I met Christ and became a Christian I was adopted into a family that loved me unconditionally. In the church I was loved. In the church I mattered.

As a result of the acceptance I received from church, which I never received at home, I threw myself into church. In the late 1990s I joined a small assembly mainly because the pastor was an excellent teacher of the Bible. I was desperate to sit under someone who knew more Bible than I did.

I WAS AT HOME

The small assembly took my wife, my son and I in with open arms and we felt at home. We were loved, prayed for, and accepted. They even invited me to teach the Bible on occasion. I made new friends and attended several Bible conferences in the area. I also developed a strong friendship with a local missionary who was trying to get a church plant going. We became very close and my family supported him and his work. Sometimes my family would be the only believers in his little church on his Tuesday night services. We shared meals together more times than I can count.

Then the unthinkable happened. My pastor left for an assembly in Arizona. The pastor who replaced him wasn't educated, nor did he know his Bible as well. He also believed that the King James was the only inspired version. I expressed my concern to the pastor in private, and he came to my home weekly to discuss the issues of inerrancy and the KJV Bible. In the meantime, I was forbidden to teach in church. Our weekly talks continued for several months until he passed away.

I thought that maybe I would now be able to teach in church again. But the problems were only just beginning.

SCANDAL ERUPTS

I didn't know my late pastor was keeping notes of our conversations. A few weeks after his death, another man in the church "discovered" these notes of our weekly meetings in the pastor's study and took them to the mid-week service where he read them out loud to the congregation. I was not present at this meeting, but the men of the church were outraged to find out what I believed. It was argued that since I no longer believed the Bible, swift action must be taken against me.

CONDEMNATION

In a unanimous vote by all the men of the church, I was condemned. The charge was heresy. I was accused and found guilty of disbelieving the very Word of God. I was not given the opportunity to defend myself. At this point, I still did not even know what had happened that night in the mid-week service.

I found out on a cold Saturday morning in December 2001 when I received a letter in the mail from my church. In it, they informed me that I had been condemned for heresy, was cast out from the church, and had been handed over to Satan. I was devastated. The church family that loved me and prayed with me, had now condemned and abandoned me. I called the man who wrote the letter, and he assured me that I could speak before the church and defend my position. He also promised that I could read the journal that our late pastor kept. Both of these have been denied me to this day.

My missionary friend also abandoned me. Though we had been close friends for many years, he could not afford to be in contact with me since he depends on the support of my former church and others like it. Maintaining fellowship with me would have put his financial support in jeopardy. I do not fault him for this, and he eventually moved to Kentucky, and now pastors a small congregation.

But I was abandoned to my fate. In southern West Virginia, word travels fast among the church community, and being a modern-day heretic was a death sentence for someone like me who wanted to enter full-time ministry. No one would come near me nor did they want me near them. I was despondent and lonely. No local church wanted my family and I to attend their services. After a while, I stopped trying to find somewhere to worship. The family of believers that I had come to know had turned out to be no different than the family that had raised me. I could excuse the family that raised me for their behavior—after all, they were not believers—but how could Christians abandon me?

JESUS

The story doesn't end there though. When abandoned by all I knew and loved, I turned to Jesus. I know that sounds simple, even obvious. However, prior to this I was always drawn to the pastor. Now that I was alone, I was forced to seek Jesus. I learned to depend on him completely and I soon found that he and his mission filled the void left by the church. I cannot bring myself to join with another assembly, even after all these years. I worship at home. My wife has never wavered in her support of my decision and me. My two sons are raised in a home surrounded by the love of God. And we let them choose which Bible translation they want to read.

REDIRECTED

I am now obsessed with Jesus and his work. I consider myself a Christ-follower. Leaving the organized church and realizing

"I am the church" has been critical in my Christian walk. Jesus has introduced me to people from all walks of life and in these meetings we share stories of what Jesus has done in our life. It is exhilarating watching someone learn about Jesus for the first time or seeing someone freed from the shackles of organized religion.

CONCLUSION

The man that led the charge to condemn me as a heretic became the pastor of my former church, and he now has a successful radio ministry. I hope he does well and that God is glorified in what he is doing. Though the experience I endured under him is painful, I look to him as the reason I am free from organized religion. In his effort to rid the church of a dangerous man and consign that man to judgment, he freed that man and enabled him to go on and live a life dedicated to Jesus and his mission.

CHAPTER 8
LEAVING CHURCH TO FIND CHURCH

By Travis Klassen

In many contexts of life, the act of departure often garners positive responses, as it evokes thoughts of travel, conquest, change, and arrival. Yet leaving a church is most often viewed negatively, as if by leaving a church, one is abandoning God or the faith. But this is rarely the case and often ignores the journey of faith through fear and trials that led up to the departure, or the eventual destination to which God is leading. Those who leave a church are usually simply following God toward a new adventure of faith and an expression of life lived in obedience to God.

Early on in my journey away from the institutional church, I made a lot of mistakes. I misdirected anger at people who I felt had hurt me, and spoke out quite loudly at the injustice of the institution that I felt had crushed me.

As time passed, and as I moved further away from the church in its traditional form, I began to see the church for who she really is: the beautiful, relational, living, breathing bride of Jesus. As I grew in this perspective, I couldn't help but grow in love for the body that Jesus loves so much.

MY JOURNEY

My wife and I had already left a church once that was "institutional" in nature, and spent a year soul-searching, writing music, and contemplating what church was really supposed to be. On any given Sunday, our fellowship with the universal church could be considered to be floundering or flourishing, depending on your perspective.

Though I had strong convictions that something was wrong, I didn't really know what it was or what do about it. We wandered alone for a year without any real spiritual direction.

While we walked through this churchless wilderness, a good friend—a leader with much charisma and drive—pursued us and convinced us to start a church with him. We'd lead worship and he'd preach. It was going to be a church like none either of us had ever been a part of. We would share meals together. There would be no paid staff. The primary goal would be relationships with God and with one another.

There would be none of the formalities that were found in traditional, institutional churches. There would be no offering time, but if people were lead to give they could bring their offering to a small box near the front of the church. There would be no printed bulletin, as we would be communicating with each other as family members do.

Worship would be free and uncontrolled, and we would just follow the direction of the Holy Spirit at any given gathering. We'd meet on a set evening and enjoy dinner together as we worshipped God and fellowshipped with one another.

Kids would stay in the gathering and learn along with the adults, experiencing real and relational church from an early age.

These were our dreams.

OUR SPLINTERED DREAMS

These were the dreams that helped us overcome our fear, and build up the courage to return to ministry and the church. In the beginning it felt as though we were living our dreams, like there was nothing missing and everything was good and right.

But these dreams were eventually crushed.

These dreams were taken away, one by one, until there was nothing left that was different from any other formalized, institutionalized church.

Pure hearts entwined in relationship with God and one another became tainted by a lust for pre-programmed fellowship times, "excellence" in worship, and well-produced Sunday services. People stopped thinking for themselves, stopped exploring their faith, and started taking it all in, attending for the experience. We chose songs and let them sing along and we preached sermons to get the people to do what we wanted. The people, as we leaders referred to them, became observers instead of active co-participants in a cooperative expression of worship.

We put on a great show and gave the people what they wanted, but in my heart I knew we weren't advancing. While it appeared we were making great strides forward, acquiring a building, building a congregation and creating a worship experience that was unrivalled in the city — I knew that the life inside, the fiery, passionate zeal was being stifled. We'd abandoned the adventurous journey of faith, and substituted a weekly ritual that felt more like a funeral, dominated by ceremony, tradition, and routine.

What began as a dream for something different gave way to a nightmare. Night after night we wondered how we went from something so pure, so organic to ... this. We wondered how we went from living the dream to dying in a nightmare.

OUR ANSWER

It has been two years since our dream died and we left the nightmare behind. I have spent those two years asking God, "What happened?"

The answer, if you can call it that, came slow. I began to realize that anything that isn't rooted in truth would still point to God, even if it seems to point away from God. Anything that exists, whether it appears beautiful or ugly, true or false, exists solely on matter created by God, and thus has at one time been judged as good.

What I began to realize is this: we were trying to build church, something only God can build, on a framework and foundation fully built and established by man. Ever heard of a the house built on sand?

It worked for a while. It was good. It was almost too good. But as with any house built on sand, cracks began to form in the foundation and walls. To patch these up, we eventually had to begin instituting rules and policies to protect church unity and peace.

From there it was the beginning of the end for our dreams.

But this was not the end for God's dream. We had to leave that church, but as we slowly climbed out of the shadowy valley, we've had some pretty amazing experiences. Some days we gain ground, and some days we fall. Sometimes we reach out, and sometimes we just hold on.

On this journey we've discovered a community of Jesus followers that is vibrant, eclectic, passionate, and more than a little bit quirky. I wouldn't trade these experiences and these intricate relationships for the world. There is a lot less structured fellowship, and we have to be intentional about our participation, but in this free-form expression we've found church in a very pure, real, and vibrant way.

I used to trivialize people who, during a particularly exciting or inspiring conversation about God, would suddenly get excited and exclaim, "This is church!" They would point out that we were the "two or more gathered in his name," and we were being the church. I used to hear from those we called rebels, from those that didn't fit in, the misfits if you will—but the phrase I used to think was so clichéd has become a regular part of my vocabulary. Realizing that we are the church, and believing it, was a breakthrough I didn't know I needed.

Whether joining a buddy after work for a beer and building each other up as we pursue to be godly men, or hearing of a financial need in our circle of friends and giving money without the expectation of a charitable receipt—this is church. Having a couple of families over for a barbecue and building healthy relationship—this is church. Stopping by the local food bank or youth shelter—this is church, this is the kingdom of heaven on earth—and this is what Jesus said he was building.

We catch glimpses of what "church" could look like, and we keep pursuing the truth in God and in community with people. I don't know if we'll ever "arrive," but I am finally okay with that. I'd rather spend more of my life journeying than arriving; for it is only on the journey we grow.

With every step further, we grow stronger. Some days we feel like we are running. On those days we see that one of the greatest advantages to living with Jesus and his followers outside of the institution is that out here there are no signs saying, "No running in church."

CHAPTER 9
NEVERTHELESS

By Tyson Phillips

To the church of my youth, the church I once loved,

These are the words of one who served you as a child, sitting on my father's lap, listening to stories about Jesus and believing that Jesus loves everyone, even the little children. I brought you my pennies every Sunday. I brought you myself every Sunday.

You taught me to believe that there is life after this life. When my grandfather died, tears dripped off the tip of my nose as I walked around the neighborhood telling my neighbors that my grandfather had died during the night. You taught me that I would see him again in a better place.

Grandfather and I had planted a huge garden together. Grandfather plowed the ground, then we made long straight rows, planted small hard seeds we had purchased from the nursery and marked the end of each row with a scrap of paper with the name of what we had planted in that row. Grandfather told me that we are like those seeds in this life, but when we're placed in the ground we too would someday spring to life and become something even more beautiful.

When I watched the snow falling outside my window on winter nights, I thought of that night when Jesus first arrived as a baby in Bethlehem. Snow reminds me of Christmas. Christmas brings gifts, but the best gift of all is Jesus. Jesus loves me this I know, for the Bible tells me so.

Nevertheless, I have this against you: When my father lay dying in the hospital, you were not there. When he died a few days later, you were not there. When I lay in my bed each night, listening to my mother sobbing herself to sleep in the next room, you were not there. When I tried to figure out why my father had died, you were not there.

You said Harold was a drunk, the "worst sinner" in town. Yet Harold was there. Harold took me with him as he made his business calls. When Harold stopped at the bar for a beer, he parked around the corner, left me in the car and brought me a bag of chips to eat and a soda to drink while he had his beer. "Don't worry," he said. "I only had one beer, so it's safe for me to drive." Mother never knew we stopped at the bar.

On Sunday morning Harold parked around the corner from the church. I slipped out near the end of the service, before the last prayer. Before the church people had finished praying, Harold and I were on our way to yet another gun show. I didn't care much about gun shows, but I knew Harold cared about me and I treasured our time together.

Even though you had money to pay for large buildings, you had no money to help our struggling family after my father died. When we almost lost our car because my mother could not make the payments you were not there. The attorney you described as a "sinner" helped us pay for our car. The doctor you said was a "Communist sympathizer" charged us reduced rates and offered to help pay for my college education. But you were not there.

When our first child died in childbirth, you were not there. When my wife almost died, you were not there. You were in a committee meeting and could not take messages. When I lay in the hospital at death's door for three days, you were not there.

Yet when the church bulletin I typed had misspellings, you were there to correct those. When my friend moved in with his girlfriend, you appeared almost immediately to advise him of his sin and to tell him that he and his girlfriend were not welcome within your walls.

Even though several of my female friends said they felt God was calling them to work with the poor, the widows, the lonely, and to "preach the Good News," you told them they were mistaken. You told them the Bible was against them, and that Satan himself was calling them to do these things. You told them their job was to obey and serve their husbands. If they had no husbands, you told them that it was "the Lord's will" that they find husbands.

When anyone dared disagree with your "interpretation" of Holy Scripture, you were there to set him or her straight. When you needed more money for buildings or staffing, you sent me letters, called on the phone and appeared at my door to explain why the "Lord needs you to give more money."

Yet you had mere pennies for the poor. You said those who lived in the streets should "get off their lazy asses and get a job." Yet you had millions for huge sanctuaries with vaulted ceilings, stained glass windows, sound systems, carved pulpits, and padded pews.

You crossed the street to avoid the homeless, the poor, and the neighbors on your way to Sunday services. You never learned their names and did not want to know them. You pretended they were not there. You put a check in the offering plate for missions in some far off land, but ignored your neighbors.

You hid in your sanctuaries from what you imagined to be the corruption of the world. You did not want to hug the filthy, invite the hungry out for lunch, welcome the broken-hearted, help single mothers who were about to be thrown out of their homes, pay a utility bill for a family that had lost their only source of income, or become polluted by the sins of the masses by getting to know them. You feared they might want something from you if they knew you.

You consoled yourself with the idea that "correct theology and a correct understanding of the Bible" was what religion was all about. You diligently searched out what you imagined to be the sins of others, yet were blind to your own. You found Bible verses that you could use against others, but skipped those that might have something to say about you. You forgot that Jesus said that if you understand what He said, you would do it.

You desired that the rich attend your banquets and your all-you-can-eat pie nights. When you learned that the new couple were both highly paid professionals, he a medical doctor and she a university professor with a Ph.D., you crowded around them by the dozens, hoping to make their acquaintance and to encourage them to attend regularly and give generously. Yet you ignored another new couple who began attending the same week. They were a racial minority and appeared poor.

You condemned every woman who had ever had an abortion from your pulpit and called them murderers. You did not know those listening to you well enough to know that you had just called several of them murderers for something they had done long ago. You did not know that they still suffered because of that past choice. You were not there after church as they ran outdoors and sobbed. You wondered aloud why they never again darkened your doors.

You called every "home-o-sex-you-all" a deviant from the pit of hell. You assumed that there were none of these deviants in your congregation, and made it clear that these deviants were not welcome within your walls. You were not there as some of the people who heard you cried themselves to sleep that night. You never understood why Andrew committed suicide. Why would such a bright young man with a promising future do such a thing?

You never understood why your neighbors hated you. If they stayed up late partying on Saturday nights and wanted to sleep in on Sunday mornings, you thought they should not complain when your amplified "Gospel music" woke them up on Sunday mornings. When your parking lots drained rainwater into their yards, you did not understand why they were angry. When you told their children to stay off your property you did not understand why they hated you.

You loved those who agreed with what you taught and told those who disagreed that they were "in serious trouble" and implied that they were not real Christians. You loved the rich, but avoided the poor. You craved property in "good neighborhoods," and sited your buildings in poor neighborhoods only because property cost less there.

You did not love your neighbors because you never made an effort to know your neighbors. You loved only those who loved you and agreed with you.

You decided that reforming the culture and electing politicians who agreed with your values, making the country a "Christian nation" was the path to bringing the Kingdom of God to earth. You overlooked what Jesus had to say about the Kingdom and how to live in the Kingdom.

You hid abuse within your ranks. You overlooked those among you who abused children within your own walls. You refused to deal with those who molested children until multi-million dollar judgments forced you to sit up and take notice. You accused those who complained of being abused and molested when they were children of fabricating stories to "cash in" on possible future court-ordered judgments. You hid your bank accounts and other assets so the court could not order you to use your money to pay former victims of your abuse.

You cared for yourself and those like you, but had no love for others. You loved your stately buildings, your golden spires, your stained glass windows, and your money, but you scorned others.

You desired my money, my time, and my attendance, but had no time for my family or me. You chased after your lovers, but abandoned your first love. You forgot what Jesus said and did, and invented a new Jesus and followed the Jesus you invented, the Jesus as you wanted him to be. Not the wild and crazy Jesus of the Gospels. Not the Jesus who loved sinners and ate with them. Not the Jesus who touched lepers. Not the Jesus who loved the poor. Not the Jesus who said to sell what we have and give to the poor. Not the Jesus who loved the Samaritans. Not the Jesus who loved women and elevated their status in society. Not the Jesus who forgave. Not the Jesus who said to forgive those who trespass against us.

Therefore I issue you this decree of divorce. I will not walk with you again. I will walk with those you scorn and with the One who walks with them. I will spend myself on behalf of the poor, the unloved, the overlooked, those who are not welcome within your walls. I will love those you hate. I will sit with them as they weep. I will touch them. I will put my arms around them. I will not miss you. I do not miss you. I understand that you never loved me. Your love was spent elsewhere.

CHAPTER 10
FOLLOWING THE GYPSY KING

By Tara Pohlkotte

I grew up as a pastor's daughter. This provided a backstage view of the good, the bad, and the indifferent aspects of church. Though my experience was not horrible or traumatizing while I was living it, growing into adulthood has shed light on my childhood experiences. I now realize the expectations placed on my brother and me solely because of our father's public status were not just or beneficial to us as people, and certainly not reflections of the type of freedom and love demonstrated by Christ.

In my father's church, everyone had a different view of what a pastor's family should look like. But one thing was certain: there was no room for less than perfect behavior. When my brother rebelled, or when I would speak out, some people felt justified in bringing their laundry list of concerns about us to my father. It grieved him to be put in a position to listen carefully to these judgments of his children cloaked as "love," and when necessary, my father would put his role of pastor aside to stand up for us as people, not just as his children. This was never received well, and often caused further rifts within the congregation. Some supported my father being able to speak upon our behalf, while others felt he was showing favoritism to us and not listening to his parishioners. Since I hate conflict, I learned quickly to keep from adding fuel to the fire of dissension. I became the perfect pastor's daughter.

THE PERFECT PASTOR'S DAUGHTER

I learned how to fulfill the role others had given me. I led programs, started Bible studies, planned lock-ins, and was the first to sign up for the worship team. I put myself forward as I wanted to be seen, not always as I was. I struggled mightily with anxiety as a girl, but no one really knew of my struggles with doubt, fear, and self-worth. I kept my doubts private because I worried that the child of the pastor not being able to place her adolescent trust and faith in her creator was not a ringing endorsement for my father as a pastor. I hid most of my fears and learned how to be broken in socially acceptable ways. I pushed down parts of myself that were not considered "Christ like." Oh, I never smoked, drank, or was loose with boys. Instead, I worried myself into insomnia, let anxiety eat away my 5'7" frame to close to 100 pounds, and became obsessed with doing the right things so I would be worthy of love and recognition.

EMPTY RELATIONSHIPS

The adults at my church didn't dig deep enough into my life to probe if the façade I had created was truthful. Or, if they had been aware, my role as a peer leader was seen as more beneficial than a girl broken by perfectionism, so they stood back, hoping I found my way. When I was a senior in high school, my father felt it was time for him to explore other places for ministry, and he stepped down from an active pastoral role. When that happened, our family's relationships with the vast majority of the congregation we had been in for 12 years ceased to exist. I couldn't help but feel like when my father no longer served a personal purpose for these individuals that we were dismissed as people.

Along with the lack of genuine relationships, it often seemed that church people were -more likely to judge others than passionately and wildly love them. They seemed to be unified more by political party and social class than by a common purpose of following Jesus to love and serve others in this world.

For these reasons, I became weary of church. This lack of genuine love, fellowship, and concern seems to be missing in most churches I have been in, and keeps me from participating regularly in church today.

RAISING MY CHILDREN

Now, as a mother of two sweet souls, who are of age to learn who this Jesus is, I am desperately seeking to provide a different vision of the man I call Savior. So I have started penning my beliefs, as I see them, hoping to share my faith, while allowing my children to explore who they are for themselves. Here is one letter, which expresses these desires for them.

> *My children,*
>
> *Your mama loves this man named Jesus, the same name you'll hear outside. And yet, like with a lot of things, names mean different things to different people. It doesn't necessarily make one right, or one wrong, just different. So when mama says she wants to share her faith in Jesus, this is what I mean.*
>
> *Your mama finds the sky her sanctuary; I make my pulpit from the tall pines. I find communion in smoky bars, broken places, with people who don't pretend. My rosary is each ten of your toes, and while my prayers may seem sporadic, my faith runs deep and comes out in whispers.*
>
> *Your mama follows the Gypsy King.*
>
> *My gypsy Jesus, he doesn't serve on a committee, a cause, or a church calendar. He roams this world just looking for people to love. And when he finds them, oh, child – how he loves them – not for their potential, but for whom they already are. He doesn't care if they seek love from a man or a woman. He doesn't care if they've signed a recall petition. He can show them love through a beauty queen or a bar scene. He doesn't want people to change; except through love.*
>
> *Never, ever for one second believe that a fictional preteen boy with a lightning bolt on his forehead is the enemy; or the scared girl with no one to turn to, who runs to boys, or to drugs to keep from despair. The*

enemy lies in each of us, that enemy named fear. That fear that tries to root out our worth, our identity, and steal our name of 'Beloved.'

It's OK to search and hold to truths, but learn that truth is fluid and a bit hard to find. And if truth doesn't change with every person you connect with, seasons you live through, tears you shed, then honey, you can bet it was never the truth to begin with.

And oh, my darling son, who already wears virtue and strength, don't stand so straight and tall in your ideals that they become idolatrous. Instead, may your back be hunched from bending low to pick up others, may your shoulders droop from carrying the weight of stories that plumb the depths of humanity.

And my sweet girl, fight to love with a passion that is scandalous. Fight the need to compete. Fight the lies that tell you you're less than what you are. Fight the pride that tells you you're better than anyone else. Lose everything. Let life wreak you good. Breathe deep. Let your surroundings sink in.

Church people can keep their Bible studies, their quick tips, and self-righteous judgments. This is not because I'm better than them, but because these things keep me bound and worried, while I watch my view of Jesus slip silently away.

Follow closely this changing figure, who slips in and out of view. When you think you catch hold of him, and are confident you speak his voice, look again that you're not clutching a mirror.

For he is a force of nature, changing with the needs of this world. He roams and wanders, healing with the dust kicked up from his feet.

For what is justice in light of mercy? Being righteous in light of grace? Laws in light of love?

So keep loving. Trying. Living. Crying. Until at last it all seems too muddled, too gray, to find where the truth ends and the world begins....

Maybe then, I pray my children we'll see a sliver of that Gypsy Kingdom.

CHAPTER 11
LEAVING FOR LOVE

By Will Rochow

"I think you should talk to someone from your own tradition." That was the final thing a senior pastor of a large church said to me after I called seeking some help. Talk to someone from my own tradition? I know what he meant; I was a Baptist and he belonged to another denomination. Perhaps I was naïve assuming that we were all a part of the same "tradition," Christ.

As the eldest son of a former Baptist pastor and missionary, I grew up in the church. In my early thirties, I became convinced that God had called me into the pastoral ministry and I made plans to go to Bible School and then to Seminary. I was very active in the church, which included volunteering as an Associate Pastor to seniors, teaching high school Sunday school classes, and leading visitation ministries in nursing homes. Later I was called to serve as a bi-vocational pastor in a small rural community while supplementing my income by working in a grocery warehouse. Then a few years later, I received a call from another church to serve as a full time pastor, which meant uprooting the family and moving to a new community.

THE CALL OUT BEGINS

It was in this latest pastoral position that I gradually began to question a lot of my theology of the church. It wasn't one specific event that led to this, but rather the culmination of several smaller events. I began questioning why we do some of the things that we do. To say that "We've always done it that way," or "It's tradition," simply didn't sit well with me. If traditions can be proven to be unscriptural, I wondered, is it right to continue in them? Given that even Jesus questioned the people of his day concerning their misuse of traditions (Matt 15:1-9), does it not follow that we too should be at least mindful of our traditions, and especially so if we have inadvertently deified them?

One such example was when a young family began coming to our church and became quite involved. They were wonderful people. Soon they began asking about membership. In our discussion, I explained our tradition of believer's baptism by immersion being a prerequisite to church membership. They informed me that they had been baptized as believers but by pouring instead of by immersion. To them, their mode of baptism was real and precious, and they simply couldn't understand our insistence on the immersion part. My teaching that the word baptism comes from the Greek, which means to "put under" or to "immerse," wasn't enough to convince them. This couple then went on to ask, why then, did Paul say that there was only "one baptism" (Eph 4:5)? Good question.

It wasn't long before families such as this one began to pull back from being involved in our little church. Our requirements were too strict and demanding. I brought up some of these concerns at a board meeting and was promptly rebuked. It was not a pretty picture, and it was made worse by the fact that my young teenage daughter was there acting as an interim church clerk and taking minutes. To this day I believe that what she saw and heard from those church leaders has tarnished her view of the church as well. At the risk of sounding facetious, I now regret having her there to hear that "love" in action.

It soon became obvious that the love of tradition was more important than the love of people. Yes, I do believe in believer's baptism by immersion, but I also believe that love trumps all doctrine. I was convinced that the church didn't want growth, unless it was a growth that led them to their utopian 1950s version of the church. Its outreach had become conditional, and as a result, their attendance and ministry was in decline. There were many other similar events that also led to my "call out" of the ministry, and out of institutional Christianity.

CHEWED UP AND SPIT OUT

In the process of trying to be all things to all people (1 Cor 9:22), and of trying to keep the unity (John 17:23; Eph 4:3), I actually became physically sick. As the saying goes, I was "burning the candle at both ends." I felt like I was chewed up and spit out. Simply put, I was suffering from burnout. There was nothing left but an empty shell of my former self, and consequently I took a medical leave of absence.

I remember our denomination's area minister and his wife coming to visit us in our home during that time. I know that they meant well, and I hold no ill feelings toward them, but in my view at that time, they were anything but helpful and simply seemed to only reinforce the "denominational rule book."

After some time I went back to the church to resume my pastoral role, but it wasn't long before I tendered my resignation. I simply could not go through the motions of "doing" church anymore. I began to see that the way we were doing church was very religious. In retrospect, this is perhaps somewhat ironic given that we often took exception from the non-Christian community that labeled us as being religious. Who were we kidding? They were right!

After the resignation we went to another church for a while. I really tried to be optimistic. I didn't want to be perceived as just another disillusioned and angry churchgoer. However, I did become a little cynical as I saw less and less relevance in the way we "did" church. Don't get me wrong, I still loved the Lord very much, but the whole institutional system just nauseated me more and more. Soon I stopped attending church altogether.

As I agonized with God over this, a few things became apparent. God had not rejected me; He simply called me out of that which He earlier called me into. God doesn't love me less because I do not go to church, nor does He love others more because they do go to church. I learned that God's call is seasonal. There is a time for everything (Eccl 3:1-8). Still, I couldn't help feeling all alone in my Christian walk. I felt shunned by the Christian community who seemed to view me as a backslider or heretic. I yearned for fellowship, for real fellowship, and not just the usual talking about the weather and last night's football game.

As I prayed about this, God seemed to give me a somewhat strange verse. It reads, "Yet I reserve seven thousand in Israel—all whose knees have not bowed down to Baal and all whose mouths have not kissed him" (1 Kings 19:18). From this I began to understand that I was not all alone in my thinking. God does have many others who love and serve Him outside the traditional institutional church. It was not long before He arranged for me to meet some of those seven thousand.

Soon my life was filled with fellowship like I had never experienced before. The fellowship was deep and meaningful. I met more and more of God's children who also no longer attended the institutional church. We met in restaurants, bars, parks, and in private homes. Wherever the Spirit would lead (John 3:18), that is where we met. There was even a water baptism (by immersion) in my hot tub as others spontaneously broke out in song. I had never experienced that before. The Spirit was moving.

I began to hear testimonies of other pastors who had also left the church, and even met some of them. Sometime later I read a couple of interesting, but disturbing statistics. According to Frank Viola "40% of pastoral resignations are due to burnout," and "1,600 ministers in all denominations across the U.S. are fired or forced to resign each month".[1] While hard to imagine, that also helped me to see that I was not alone.

LOVE: THEOLOGY'S NEW PREREQUISITE?

So why did I leave the institutional church? Though I've asked myself that question many times over the years, the longer I am away from the institution, the less it is an issue. It has become totally irrelevant. Whenever I look at the institutional church, all I see is religion. And the very thing one would assume to be associated with the church, genuine love and relationships, I

---

1   Viola, Frank and George Barna, *Pagan Christianity?* Carol Stream: Tyndale, 2008.

personally have seldom encountered there. Granted, some will no doubt think differently about their church experience, and if so, then I will not argue. But for me there was just too much pseudo-love and conditional acceptance.

I remember my father once saying that it was too bad that I wasn't pastoring in a different church, for my experience may have been very different. While that is true, I still maintain that I was in exactly the place that God wanted me at the time. None of those experiences were mistakes. As difficult as they were, each one led me to some amazing revelations concerning the church and to the place that I am at today. For that, I thank God.

Though that is a part of my story, I prefer not to dwell on it. Contrary to what some might think, I'm not angry at the church. I would rather move on than cast stones. Whatever our church background, maybe we all should just live and let live. What does it matter if this Christian or that Christian thinks a little differently than you or I do? The more we keep focusing on our differences, the more we will fracture the body of Christ. Isn't it splintered and divided enough already? So what is the answer?

The one thing that has become more and more clear to me since my exodus from the church is that one really cannot properly discuss theology without first starting with love. Put another way, genuine and unpretentious love must be a prerequisite for any real theological study. Without learning to properly love one another first, theological study is like trying to learn about the love of Jesus from an atheist; a key element is missing. I am convinced that, if God really is love, then any study of God must be done within the framework of love. Furthermore, if I haven't first learned to love others, for whom Christ also died, then any profession of love that I may make toward God is nothing more than a lie (1 John 4:7-21). And if that is true, as I believe it is, then any theological study without the prerequisite of love is nothing more than worldly hypocrisy and may not be worth the paper it's written on. Any such study then becomes only a religious exercise at best. I find myself wanting more than just a weekly religious exercise.

They didn't teach me that in seminary. My years in the pastoral ministry didn't teach me that either. I think God had to actually call me out from the institutional church in order to reveal that truth to me. While the church may have given lip service to love, in truth there are too many traditions and denominational rulebooks that cloud what is really important. Instead of reaching out in love we were preoccupied with baptismal modes and with who could and couldn't join the church in membership. Instead of reaching out in love, we slandered and fought each other behind the scenes and in our church board meetings.

Occasionally I've been asked if I would ever go back to church. Though tempted to say never, I am open to the leading of the Spirit. I believe that if God has that in mind for me, he will also put the same calling into my wife's heart. I do not believe that God would ever call one half of a marital union without also calling the other half. That is my "Gideon's Fleece" by which I will discern God's will in this matter. At the time of this writing, the call to return to church has not come.

CHAPTER 12
A RECOVERING DRUG ADDICT

By Brian Swan

A potent drug was pumping through my veins as I attended an evangelical mega-church. The years flew by, and as a church-going Christian, I found myself deeply lost in a realm absent of truth, love, and community. The love being taught from the pulpit was not about Christ himself, it was merely about getting to know him personally by gathering more and more knowledge about him. This love of gathering knowledge was an addictive drug, and one I soaked up with my entire being.

I was what some would consider a mature Christian, showing my spiritual awesomeness among the halls of a man-made institution. I was accepted and I loved it. I was finally satisfying a craving in my heart of belonging to a loving community. I was a full-blown member, a facilitator of a strenuous discipleship class, a 10% "tither" (on gross income of course), about to step in as the leader of a 40-family adult Bible fellowship class, a minister to prison inmates every Thursday night for four years, a small group coordinator, a person on the senior pastor's research team, and an accountability partner. I attended numerous Bible and precept studies, took so many different type of leadership classes I cannot even begin to count, and I also became fluent in "Christianese." With all that filling my plate, I still found room to eat more by attending the Sunday morning worship concert (I mean service).

I was on the road to becoming what a Christian should be, informed to take on the non-church-attending infidel. Also, with God on my side, I was sure to become an elder. I looked forward to that day with great anticipation. But Christ had different plans. He led me to chuck the whole thing, and I have no intention of ever returning to religion. I wish I had a clear and concise explanation for why I left the institutional church, but it was such a complex puzzle with many moving parts, I barely understand it all myself.

RECOGNIZING MY ADDICTION

Vacationing high in the mountains of Colorado was a turning point in my life that rocked my indoctrinated soul. Either the altitude got to me, or Christ decided to jackhammer some sense into my thick skull. I was a complete ass to be around that week. I tried to be friendly and do things with my family and in-laws, but being so fixated on what was going on internally I yearned to just be alone with my thoughts, and regretfully treated others with disrespect. My head felt like it was hovering above my shoulders. I had a difficult time trying to collect my thoughts as I processed my entire institutional life over the past decade. As the week progressed, my mind would continue to churn and chew all the doctrines, rules, traditions, and verses that were pounded into my brain since becoming a Christian. After we left for home, I thought the fog would lift, but was I mistaken.

My internal soul was coming in for a crash landing. It was like base-jumping off the side of a spiritual cliff. One day, I completely lost it, and threw my discipleship workbook against the wall. As tears rolled down my face, my mind became completely clear. The tears were like little droplets of fog draining from my head. I have never taken any mind-altering drugs, but at that precise moment I could tell you what it felt like for an addict to realize they have a major problem, and is ready to seek help to remedy the situation.

My thoughts pondered Christianity as a religion, and point-by-point, I began to reject all the man-made dogma that had permeated my eyes and ears over the years. Where certainty and Bible knowledge once reigned, doubt now coursed through my veins, overpowering the indoctrination that used to flow freely. With my head no longer clogged, I could hear a voice trying to rinse, lather, and repeat a question that needed an answer: **Why do you do the things you do?**

Over and over, this question sounded, pounding the back of my eyes like a migraine headache. Why? Why? Why are there sermons, pastors, worship leaders, tithing, expensive buildings, youth groups, huge maintenance costs, interest payments, communion with stale little wafers, prayer requests, coffee shops, bookstores, a stage, decision counselors, altar calls, conventions, seminars, and a hierarchy that must be followed? Nowhere in the decade of reading and studying Scripture did I ever come across any of this "stuff."

During that decade of Bible studies and church attendance, I was a "Jesus Knowledge Freak." I loved Jesus "the knowledge," not Jesus "the person." For many years various pastors injected me with a "Jesus knowledge" drug, and I can honestly tell you this drug is addictive as crack cocaine. I was an addict and the pastors were the drug pushers. With a syringe barrel full of different topics week in and week out, the pastor would slowly place the needle with "this is how to live," and push the plunger down with "this is how to feel good" sermons. Then, as the drug coursed through my being, I would crave more. All the other addicts around me would spout more studying, more reading, and more learning. I was completely hooked on the knowledge of Christ. I was giving my entire self, as I was taught to do, to Jesus knowledge. I kept coming back for more. The institution needs a return customer, and that is exactly what they got out of me for many years.

If the person addicted to the "love of knowledge" drug misses a few church services, or has time away from studying and reading, they get the shakes or some other form of withdrawal. On the mountains in Colorado, I went through withdrawal. At first I blamed the altitude for my fuzzy head, but it was my addiction telling me the drug was wearing off. I needed a Bible hit, and I needed it now.

But admitting I was an addict was the first step toward breaking free from the love of knowledge, and finding again the love of Jesus. For the first time in my spiritual life I was seeing Christ for who he is, not the knowledge fed from the pulpit and injected into me by every program the institution sold. Most of the people I hung around were all knowledge-consuming drug addicts. The drug we all ate, drank, snorted, and smoked together kept us all on a spiritual high and gave us a false sense of relationship and community. The institution did the job it was created to do. The system kept our butts in the pews, our heads in the books, and us always looking for the next fix (or study). We were soulless, supporting a self-serving entity. As long as our addictions were fed, everything went smoothly. We were happy for every new fix, and the institution was happy to provide it.

The so-called "community" titled "church" produced a group of people who suffered more and more. Addicts will do anything to get more drugs for themselves, while helping and loving others less. With the pastor as the drug pusher, and the passive audience as the addicts, the man-made institution ran the show. The institution that runs "church" could be compared to a modern-day oil or drug cartel. A drug cartel is organization developed with the primary purpose of promoting and controlling drug trafficking. So, if the drug of choice is "Jesus knowledge," and not his actual Body, this makes the institutional church a knowledge cartel, or an indoctrination organization developed with the primary purpose of promoting and controlling the "knowledge of Jesus."

I needed out. I needed to detoxify. I needed Christ.

DELIVERANCE FROM ADDICTION

Detoxification was not an easy process. As with any drug, breaking free of addiction required months of blood, sweat, and tears. The guilt I felt was overwhelming. The condemnation I received from other addicts was immense. Worst of all, the siren song of the institutional system kept calling me back in. It took well over six months to detoxify, and it was one of the most difficult things I have ever done. The power of fear and guilt is nothing to mess around with.

The system kept trying to wrap me up with the guilt that was planted in my brain. Yet once I finally yanked away from the man-made guilt magnet, I found another magnet to cling to, the

One that holds the entire universe together. I found the magnet called Christ. Community was found outside the system.

So, here I am, wandering around in a post-institutional wilderness. It is a scary place to be, but I have never felt freer in my entire life. There is no indoctrination of "knowledge drugs," no guilt, just love.

TRUE COMMUNITY

I do not know if I was always in the wrong place at the wrong time when partaking in "church," but from my decade of experience I hardly received any sort of community beyond the surface. Nobody ever opened up his or her heart to others to reveal what was inside. No loving relationships were built. But when I left "church," I found true community with others who were outside the system. I witnessed genuine love and care among others. Most of all, I came to see and understand the love and community of Christ that I had always longed for and needed. The danger of the Jesus drug is that people think they are getting Jesus when in fact they are not. Instead, they are fed a cheap, addictive substitute, which does nothing to quench our true desire for community with Christ and with others.

Studying and learning about Christ is not a bad thing in and of itself, and I am not judging the motives of pastors and others. But when you drop everything in life to seek Jesus as knowledge, and consume a man-made Jesus product, one day a quiet moment will creep upon you and whisper the most dangerous question of all: ***Why do you do the things you do?***

Be careful pondering that question. It can be hazardous to your "system."

CHAPTER 13
LEAVING CHURCH IN THE AGE OF SOCIAL MEDIA

By Genevieve Thul

The tinny, out-of-tune piano complemented the pastor's deep bass in my earliest memories of a fundamentalist church that met at one of the parishioner's beauty salon. The sermons were long and there was a lot of Greek and Hebrew thrown around. Underneath the very intellectual façade of this church was a dark underside of deceit, power, and elitism that grew directly out of our pastor's house. Walking away wounded fit with everything else I did at eighteen, leaving for college and forging ahead to start my own life. I never even felt the scab when it tore off.

MY FAMILY'S CHURCH

I attended every denominational church I could think of as part of religious studies at school. None seemed any healthier, or any more interested in living out the truth of the Bible. I soon gave up, and announced my "personal" faith to the secular world I was surrounded by. It wasn't until the birth of my first child that I stepped through church doors again. My husband and I agreed that we wanted to raise our children in church, even though we both carried wounds from a painful past in the sanctuaries. My parents are strong Christians, and it was easy to follow their lead and become members at their church without ever researching the denomination or church history. We were initially content with the topical Sunday sermons that seemed to speak to our daily lives, and enjoyed the lively theology-based Bible studies on Wednesday nights. Slowly, those Bible studies gave way to worship nights, the Bible verses read on Sundays dwindled to one or two, and communion became something of the past. In an attempt to remain connected to the biblical basis for church, my husband accepted an invitation to join the church's leadership training, a biblical training method for training up lay leaders from the pews. They said, "Every man a minister." We took the hook—but felt the sting this time.

We became small group leaders for a struggling group of three couples. I was deep into my studies to complete my doctoral degree, and along the way, I was diagnosed with cancer. Our path became infinitely rockier as the months went by—cancer treatment for me, a horrific miscarriage, and a daughter who developed a life-threatening brain infection. At each point along the way, we stopped to examine our hearts, pray, and seek God's guidance as we questioned how we should live through this difficult time. My parents and our friends were supportive, and somehow I managed to keep up with my degree program through the toughest of life stages.

THE PAIN OF LIFE AND CHURCH

We knew trouble was on the horizon, but it didn't sneak up on us; it hit full force. Our medical bills were skyrocketing, and we felt that a second income was the responsible reaction. Yet the pastors of our church refused to write a favorable reference letter for an online teaching position I was seeking at a Christian college. We were floored when one pastor leveled his "opinion" on us: our health and financial struggles stemmed from my decision to seek further education and employment. If I hadn't "abandoned" or "neglected" our household and been a "true Proverbs 31 woman," none of this would have happened. It was obviously (in their eyes) punishment from an angry God.

The next few days were confusing. We shared the pastor's comments with my parents, siblings, and our small group members, believing that without counsel, plans fail, but with many advisers they succeed (Prov 15:22). My husband spent the summer meeting the pastor to talk over our take on the suffering in our lives and to try to reach an agreement about my God-given gifts and right to exercise them, while still tending my home. Although he made no progress, we felt we had reached an "agree to disagree" position with the pastor. But then the pastors teamed up with a good friend of ours and surprised us in our home to chastise us. With the humor of hindsight, we now call that the "pastor posse." Three weeks of bitter meetings took place, and we finally sent a short e-mail to the pastors telling them we were going to seek a new church home.

We knew there would be fall-out from this decision, but we had no idea how bad things would get. It started with phone calls, e-mails and letter from our friends encouraging us to repent and return to the church. We were stunned that many of our friends believed in a "plant your flag and die there" philosophy of church membership. We had never signed up for that. We thought we were making the decision to leave our church and find another. It came as a total surprise when we received document after document from the pastors detailing our personal lives and past sins—even some from my teen years—discrediting us and weakening our testimony. These documents were shared first with our closest friends, and finally with the whole church. In the end, we didn't leave church—we were excommunicated.

SOCIAL SLANDER

In an era of social media, being shunned by a large group is perhaps even more painful than it has been in the past. We were newcomers to our rural home, and all the friends we had were at that church. We expected to lose some, but not all. Yet as the weeks went by, I grew used to opening up my computer to check Facebook, and finding that I had been unfriended or blocked by a dozen or so friends overnight. People stopped by my blog to make hurtful comments. I continued to receive e-mails that were increasingly condemning and painful. I felt as though the whole world was watching as our good family name went up in flames.

It wasn't until I opened up a book on unhealthy churches—a mainstream book that took on cultish groups like the Moonies and Krishnas — and found my old church listed there that I began to allow myself to feel relief for our ejection from that unhealthy place. The most painful part of the process was watching my children lose every one of their friends, and having to explain that it was because we chose to question our pastor and leave our church. Finally, after reading about the denomination in the book on unhealthy churches, I was able to see how much better off my children would be without this church influencing their young lives.

A year has passed since we left our old church. We've attended two churches sporadically, large congregations where we can blend in while we heal. It has been most difficult for our children, who long for the day we finally settle into a community again. It's been difficult not to give in to their pleading, but this time we are going to research, meet with the pastor and the board, and observe for some time before we reach our decision. We know pain is inevitable in this fallen world, but we also believe that God is greater than any of it. We lean hard on Hosea 6:1 (ESV): *"Come, let us return to the Lord. He has torn us, that He may heal us; He has struck us down, and He will bind us up."*

SIX LESSONS LEARNED

I learned a few things through this difficult process of being excommunicated, and I hope others who face similar situations will find help in what I have learned.

1. **It is not unusual to be shunned by your old church.** Many authors have recorded this phenomenon. It is a self-preservation mechanism that protects the fallacies of the church you're leaving. It may not even be personal — they just need to make sure you don't have any influence that could lure other church members away.

2. **If you use social media, be prepared to proactively decrease your circle of friends to protect your family.** When our church excommunicated us, they used my blog posts, Facebook statuses, and Tweets to make a case against us. You may either need to be totally silent

about your pain on social media outlets, or block/remove people who may use your words against you.

3. **Don't get bogged down trying to defend your every thought or action.** I had to pray without ceasing and ask for the Holy Spirit's constant conviction so that I knew I was not lashing out emotionally. If I didn't feel convicted, I had to let it go. God will guide your steps when you can no longer rely on the perceptions of people who are attacking you to tell you if you are following the Lord's will or not.

4. **Make a list of people you can still call friends.** Over the years, I gathered a small list of friends from outside my church family whom I could still call for love, support, and a listening ear. I posted my list on my microwave — somewhere I would see it often. Your list will help assuage the pain of the many friends you've lost and help you realize that you are not an evil or unlovable person.

5. **Help your children develop friendships outside the church.** This was a challenge for our family because we homeschool. Our homeschool group was at our old church. Since leaving, my children have joined a sport, a 4-H club, and I have set up numerous play dates with neighborhood children. This protects them from losing all their friends again should we ever go through a similar experience at church.

6. **Develop a list of things you *did* learn at your old church, and commit to loving and praying for the people who hurt you.** Just as we are able to learn good life principles in the middle of the worst trials, so we can learn good Biblical truths at unhealthy churches. Making a list of these principles helped me salvage some good memories from this painful period, and redirected my sorrow into praise that God is big enough to overcome the flawed human church. First Corinthians 13:13 says, *"These three remain, faith, hope and love. But the greatest of these is love."* Choosing to love the people who have wounded you will help you stay close to God, and will

teach your children how to deal with pain in a Godly way. It will also build up your testimony with those around you if you are able to be charitable about a bitterly painful experience.

SECTION 2
SWITCHING CHURCH

I have done a lot of church hopping. When my wife and I lived in Wheaton, we attended a mega church for a while, and got involved with teaching in their children's program, but the church was somewhat liturgical, and we wanted to find a church that was a little less structured. We found another church in town that fit what we were looking for, and attended there before we moved to Denver.

In Denver, my wife and I visited over 60 churches. We were hyper critical of all churches at this time. One church was too Calvinistic. At another, they spent too much time teaching from Rick Warren, and not enough time from the Bible. In one, the music was too loud; it another the music went too long. In one, I didn't like the preaching; in another there was no preaching. We finally ended up joining a new church plant, but soon left this church also to return to Montana and become a pastor for the first time.

Even as a pastor, I switched churches. I briefly wrote about this in Section 1. I loved pastoral ministry, and always joked that I was the only pastor I could bear to listen to. Today, I am not sure that this is so funny.

When we lived in Dallas, we went back to church hopping. Dallas is the mega church capital of the world, but we vowed to stay away from such churches, as we thought they only catered to the whims of culture. But after visiting dozens of churches over the course of two years, we landed in a mega church. Why? The preaching was fantastic. The problem was that we had to drive 45 minutes to get to church, and it was difficult to get involved in any meaningful way.

So, much like in Denver, we ended up joining a new church plant near where we lived. It was Mosaic Arlington. The pastor, Stephen Hammond, was one of the most genuine, loving, creative, and insightful pastors I have ever met. And the people in the church reflected this. What is more, it was right about this time that I got fired from my job in Dallas (as I shared in the previous section on Leaving Church). The people in this church banded around us with love and care. People brought over food. Stephen invited me along with him to minister to homeless people and ex-convicts. I still remember driving around town in his Jeep, with "Hotel California" and "Viva la Vida" blasting from the speakers.

At the same time, I was also preaching at a little Hispanic church in another part of town. Most of the people in this church were dirt poor, but when I lost my job, they banded around us with genuine love and support. They provided job leads to help me find work. One man gave us $100 one Sunday. Others invited us over for meals and one young family loaned us a car.

Looking back, I am so thankful to God for these two churches. If I had been attending that mega church 45 minutes away, I sincerely doubt that anyone would have known about our struggles. Their ignorance would not have been their fault. We were too far away to actually get to know anyone. But by switching from the mega church to Mosaic Arlington and the little Hispanic church, God placed us with a group of people who could band around us in our time of deepest need.

Despite my current views on church and following Jesus, I believe that if we still lived in Dallas, my family and I would still be involved in both of these churches. While I believe that Jesus is currently calling my family to follow him outside of the four walls of the traditional church, I believe that if we were still in Dallas, Jesus would be calling us to participate in ministry with the people of these two local churches.

I share all this to show that while people who switch churches sometimes get a bad rap from pastors and ministry leaders, the truth is that sometimes people jump from one church to another because God is leading them to do so. Sometimes, God brings a family to a church for a particular period of time simply because God wants to teach something to that family (or to the church) during that time. Then God leads them elsewhere. Churches and ministry leaders should not get upset at this, for if it is true that we are all part of one Body of Christ, then people really do not go from one "church" to another, but simply move from one portion of the Body to another.

The stories in the following chapter reveal this theme. The people who write these stories write about where they have attended church, why they left their church, and what God taught them as they moved from one church to another.

CHAPTER SUMMARIES

Through a series of attending numerous churches over the span of several years, Shannon Brisco came to recognize that change in churches comes slow, but often the change we want to see in our church may actually be the change God wants to accomplish in our own life instead.

Jessica Bowman contrasts mass-produced factory food with fresh, healthy, organic food, and shows how there is a parallel to both in the ways we approach Jesus, God, and church. Now that she is feasting on the natural Jesus, she will never return to the artificial, additive-filled church from which she came.

Lauren LaRue has experienced all the ups and downs of church life. She has led successful ministries in a thriving church, been condemned and outcast by a judgmental church, has sought to help new churches get established, and help dying churches make the necessary changes to survive. Her story is full of pain and frustration, but contains hope for the future. If you have faced troubles in church, you will resonate with Lauren's story.

Kellen Freeman spent many years looking for a church that fit his desire for good preaching, quality music, and ministry options he could plug into. Then he discovered that all he really wanted and needed is a church family. He realized that if he could find that, he could find church anywhere, regardless of denomination, worship style, or church size.

Eric Hatfield has been in numerous types of churches with numerous different practices and beliefs. He shows how God has used all these experiences to teach him how to depend on God and work in unity with other Christians.

Many people have experienced the fear and frustration of attending a church where the pastor is hungry for power and control. Wayne Hobson has experienced this, and shares why he and his wife left such a church. However, this did not keep them away from church altogether. They eventually found a church where the pastors were warm, loving, and trusting.

Kimberly Parker made a commitment to attend her church and serve faithfully. Two and a half years later, she found herself leaving that church. She explains why and how she made this difficult decision to change churches, and how you also can find guidance in your life if you are facing a similar choice.

Felisa Reed never felt at home in church until she found an eclectic group of people who were open and honest about their doubts and fears, who accepted people from all beliefs, and who helped each other through their trials and failures. Felisa writes about how she found this community, and why she finally feels at home.

With beautiful and heart-touching storytelling, Sam Riviera shows us what the church really looks like, and how we can live and serve in the Kingdom of God through daily actions of love and care toward those around us and toward those who may not get love from anybody else. If you want to know how to live in the Kingdom of God, this chapter will inspire and challenge you.

Cara Sexton writes about the common struggle so many Christians face in trying to find the perfect church—such a church doesn't exist. She discovered that she couldn't find church in a building until she found it in herself.

CHAPTER 14
CHURCH CHANGE

By Shannon Brisco

I grew up surrounded by church change, and I don't mean the collection plates. I mean some pretty big shifts from one church to another in a variety of ways: denomination, location, language, dress code, views towards mission and social justice, worship style and liturgies. The majority of the people that I encountered in most of those church and Christian circles fell into one of two categories: they were absolutely convinced that "their" way was the right way to "do things" and that people who chose to do things differently were somehow off base; or they were oblivious to the possibility that there was any other way of doing things.

DIFFERENCES

I grew up in a Pentecostal Church in the middle to upper class suburbs. My parents were involved in the worship ministry and both of my grandparents had been ministers/evangelists. We always got dressed up for church and, at that time, went to a morning and evening service. We'd have communion once a month where we sat in our seats and the crackers and grape juice were passed along the pews. There were a lot of hymns and new worship choruses, a baptismal service maybe once a year, and the occasional missions focus Sunday where missionaries would visit and share stories from Kenya or some other faraway place. Most of the church ate lunch at a nearby restaurant, part of a chain we called "Christian Chicken." (I don't know if it's just a Pentecostal thing or a Canadian thing.) This was simply how church was done. During this time, I was attending a very strict, fundamentalist Christian school and my friend from school invited me to go with her to her church one Sunday. I woke up on Sunday morning, got dressed and when I walked into the kitchen her mom's first comment was, "Where's your hat?"

"Huh? Hat? You don't wear a hat to church..." I thought. As I awkwardly put on a hat they let me borrow and arrived at church, I realized I would have been almost the only female without a hat had I not accepted their offer. But does what we wear when we go to church matter to God? We don't dress to impress God.

Worship styles are something else that I used to talk about and consider as an important factor for where I went to church. Many people today use musical preferences to help determine where they attend church. One church doesn't sing enough hymns, another sings too many. In one church, the music is too loud; in another, it is not loud enough. Then there are the churches that sing love songs to Jesus as if he were my boyfriend, while other churches sing with almost no emotion whatsoever. Of course, most music can be worshipful if we focus on the message of the song rather than the tempo or volume of the music, and sing the words as a prayer to God rather than as a reflection of our own desires. This is when music is honoring to him and brings us closer in fellowship with him.

Then there is liturgy. Liturgy is a term I never heard until I started attending a Presbyterian Church and noticed some differences to what I had been accustomed to seeing and experiencing in church. I now know that every church has a liturgy, even the Pentecostal church I grew up with. Liturgy is simply a style and practice of worship that follows a particular pattern. However, some of the practices of the Presbyterian Church, being new to me, seemed to be much more intentional. I'd never seen a pastor wear vestments before. I had always had some misconception that only religious officials in the Catholic Church wore those. I had never encountered written prayers, which were read during services. And I'd never gotten out of my seat for communion. In the beginning I was very uncomfortable and felt like I was attending a church that somehow did things wrong. But I soon recognized that their practices weren't wrong — just different.

The way I dress or the style of music I like doesn't help me get to know others. These things only reflect my personal preferences. People get to know each other by spending time together, having conversations about life, and sharing with one another in joys and trials. Why should it be any different with God? I feel that a lot of churches focus too much on how to do things the right way, rather than focusing on building the Jesus relationship and supporting the journey as a community of believers.

DEPARTURE

For a period of time I pushed away from church altogether. I just didn't feel like I was being authentic. I felt like I was going through a bunch of motions that I had been taught, which were "Christian-like" but I didn't feel it in my heart. I attended a liberal Christian university and found myself rarely going to church. But I was engaging in meaningful dialogue for the first time about how the Christian faith intersects with social justice and reaching out to those who were in need. This rang true to my ears and aligns with so much of Scripture. I felt new life was breathed into my beliefs.

What did my faith call me to do? How am I to be different as a result of who I am in Christ, and what is my purpose as a Christian? Although this may have been an intended message behind what previous churches and pastors had tried to communicate, it was different when I caught a glimpse of the reality in the words.

RETURN

I started attending a Mennonite Church, although not regularly. At first I was really hesitant because I had pictured people pulling up in a horse and buggy, wearing bonnets, and having really delicious potlucks. However, what I experienced was quite different. It was a community of believers from all walks of life—rich and poor, black and white, old and young—which met on a weekly basis to learn about the character and person of God, to learn about His purpose for their lives, and how they could be a witness and an encouragement in practical ways to needy people around them. This was something that I could embrace. These people didn't put on an act and their Sunday "best" to see each other on Sundays. They lived life in community, in transparency and openness, and in fellowship with other people who were also figuring out and taking their faith day-by-day. Where had this type of church been my whole life? This seemed to be the type of community I was looking for. It had no pretenses, and no fake smiles when life became difficult. It was an actual community of believers who walked alongside each other in both spiritual and practical ways.

Through a series of events, I ended up moving again to a very liberal part of Canada. There weren't many churches in this area at all, let alone anything that resembled the Mennonite Church I had previously attended. I first connected with a small church after being invited to a small group Bible study hosted at a young couple's house. They welcomed me genuinely from the first day I attended and conversation flowed naturally. They invited me to visit their church, which rented out a school on Sundays. The church was equally friendly, actively involved in reaching out to serve people in their community (through free finance counseling and tax help to food basket deliveries to families in need), and they worshiped God with a variety of music, prayers, and practical sermons.

When it came time for me to move once more, a group of my church friends showed up and spent the day working hard to help me pack up. This group of people practiced what they preached—they loved me for who I was and where I was at and invited me into their community to live and learn about God together.

After this move, I started attended a large church. It met in an old Catholic Church building that had been renovated on the inside. It was always packed to capacity with a congregation of mostly younger people in their 20s to 40s. The pastor gave amazing practical sermons week-after-week, which I found almost always applied directly to a situation in my life at the time. He used video clips and references to current social trends or situations within the community and society at large that we could all relate to and understand. I could certainly apply this to my life and I felt that through his sermons I was growing to learn more about God. God was increasingly real, present, and not at all far removed. I didn't have to study theology and understand deep doctrines to start to build my relationship with Him. It was like a burden was lifted and I was seeing my God for the first time in a new light. And although I've now lived in another part of Canada for three years, I still continue to download that pastor's weekly sermon podcasts.

Most recently, I have been working for a Christian non-profit organization, which, although not a church, really feels, like my extended Christian family. They too practice what they preach, and not in a judgmental, harsh, or critical way. They simply live what they teach. Their lives are an example of what they believe and talk about. We have regular chapels where we sing worship songs, which speak to the character and holiness of God. We have times of joint prayer where we spend time praying for our country, our government (regardless of politics), and world issues of peace, hunger, AIDS, and other major concerns. We have times of laughing, games, fellowship, and food. We grieve losses together and share in the joys of new beginnings and exciting news. I was sick once for about a week and my manager and a few directors sent e-mails and text messages to see how I was doing and to ask if I needed anything. The HR Director showed up with a care package with goodies of soup, fruit, oatmeal, and throat lozenges. These people live the way Christians should.

CHURCH CHANGE IS SLOW

If you are looking for changes in your church, recognize that change may take place over a long period of time and there may be several steps to the process. It may be that you are the one who will change. But that is part of the journey.

Nobody is perfect. No church is perfect because a church isn't a building, it's a group made up of imperfect people. However I think that striving to understand and be serious about what we believe and why and how it is part of our day-to-day life is the key to practical faith. Learning about God, spending time with Him, living in community with others to share experiences and the journey that is called life — that is what church is all about.

CHAPTER 15
FROM FACTORY-FARMED GOD TO GRASS-FED JESUS

By Jessica Bowman

Our journey into leaving church, like that of most people, was a long time in coming. We stayed out of obligation, we stayed out of guilt, we stayed for our own gain (for ministry references), but in the end, the Spirit led us to an understanding that we couldn't rely on an institution to provide what only God could give and that sometimes the spiritual grass really is greener on the other side.

We spent years committed to the institution of church, dedicated to the largest denomination in America; we were born and bred into it. My husband grew up as an MK (missionary kid) and I was your stereotypical girl from a broken family who found acceptance and reprieve in my local youth group.

But then adulthood happened and along with it, brokenness, renewal, and grace. The glimpses of Jesus that we thought we had seen in the traditional church as children faded away until we couldn't find it at all. The Jesus that we had found in graduating from milk to meat was missing in the church. Forget an all you can eat spiritual buffet; we were handed hard mash and gruel in the form of hyper-conservatism and legalism. And it tasted bad.

LEARNING TO COOK AGAIN

We noticed this years before we actually pushed away from the table. We thought maybe we could be the change we wanted to see, from within the church. We thought we could get into the leadership kitchen and bring to light simple, refreshing spiritual recipes from our favorite Book. We thought we could bring back the old, good-for-the-soul favorites that had long been forgotten and do away with the recipes for success that were filled with too many additives and fake ingredients.

What we found is that Christians are the pickiest eaters around. They don't like trying new things, even if you can prove that they're healthier and have more natural ingredients. Most Christians want what they're used to, what they've always known—even if it's bad for them.

Even so, we were afraid to leave, to cook in our own kitchen. We were afraid of not being understood, of being shunned, mistrusted, and labeled. We desperately wanted to collaborate. We wanted partnership and support. We lacked faith to "do" ministry outside of an organization.

But it finally reached a point where we could no longer stay in the institution of cooking up Jesus with artificial sweeteners and harmful preservatives. Our souls could no longer bear to serve Jesus in a box, no matter how professional the packaging. There were just too many cooks in the kitchen. Too many knives … too many backs. And so, finally, we left.

And that is where we found the freedom we had always suspected should be found in Christ, the freedom that we had been reading about in our favorite Cookbook all those years, the bread and the wine that we had been hungering for, the fruit, and the seeds, and the streams of living water to wash it all down with. And it tasted sweeter. More natural. Healthier.

Not perfect, mind you. Embracing a community model of consuming Jesus is tricky. Even in its simplicity, it is complicated. Why? Because mutual edification and grace are substances that most of us aren't used to cooking with. We're used to consuming. We're used to having The Father cooked up for us and served on pretty china, in small, manageable bites, or worse, in bottles.

Learning to cook, and serve unto others, as you would have them cook and serve unto you, takes practice. It takes faith, goodness, knowledge, self-control, perseverance, godliness, brotherly kindness and love. And if these ingredients aren't used in increasing measure, The Body suffers from spiritual malnutrition. It becomes bloated on its own ineffectiveness.

So, yes, embracing the fine art of sowing seeds in your own front yard and gathering cooks in your own kitchen won't be without its ups and down, it's trials and errors. Not all seeds spring forth. Weeds infiltrate. Pests creep in to destroy. No garden is perfect (well, except for that original one). But life will prevail. Life in the Son grows, regardless of the weather. It takes root and it multiplies when properly tended to.

FIND FULFILLMENT IN JESUS

If you're in an institution that doesn't seem to satisfy, that isn't cooking up the recipes you know to be true and good, don't be afraid to listen to the Spirit within you. The Spirit that tells you there's more to being the church. Jesus may be hard to chew sometimes, but he is always good. He is the only thing in this world that can sustain and satisfy your appetite for love and fulfillment.

Be sure, freedom from a lifetime of artificial Jesus presented on a legalistic platter is only part of the reward available to us in this life. The real prize is recognizing the joy in the journey. It's learning how to look up into the Son, to feel his warmth and goodness on your face, and recognize him as the life-giver, the plant-grower, the rain-dropper — and then allowing his Spirit to teach you how to take all these individual ingredients of grace, and cook a masterpiece of love that not only nourishes your own soul but can also be served to the Body.

People are hungry. They're starving. And no amount of factory-farmed Jesus will satisfy them, though it may give them spiritual cancer or trick their brain into thinking that what they're consuming is sweet on the tongue. But we, the called-out ones, know better. We know that spiritual food is real and that the Body can only be nourished when filled with entrees grown, harvested, and prepared from God's own garden.

So seek him. Seek his truth, his light, his Spirit, and his Son. And then be willing to follow him down new-to-you paths of the garden if that's what it takes to find the healing that can only come from being indwelled with the Creator of all things.

CHAPTER 16
WHAT IS "CHURCH," ANYWAY?

By Lauren LaRue

I discovered the love of Christ one night alone on my living room floor. Behind on the rent, jobless, and desperate, I had exhausted all sources of help and reached up to Christ. Even though I was not raised in a church-going family there had been various people throughout the years who had witnessed to me. It was their words that I recalled when I sank to my knees that night. "Jesus come into my life. Forgive me for my sins. Take over my life because I am doing such a terrible job at this." I experienced the love of Christ in such a way that I would never be the same. One moment I felt filthy, and the next I knew I was loved and accepted. No other love has consumed me so completely.

I began to read a Bible my brother had given me, and to my surprise the words came alive! My heart was filled with a burning desire to know my Savior more. Several months went by, and as my heart and life were being transformed, I knew I needed the help and support of a church. I had grown up in an abusive environment, and as an adult I was co-dependent, and afraid to be alone. I went from one bad relationship to another until I had a child. Then I clung desperately to a man I did not love out of fear that no one would want me. He was mean to me, he cheated on me, and I wanted out of the relationship so I could learn to become a good mom and teach my daughter independence. I though church would help me accomplish this.

DIVORCING CHURCH

The church I chose was a Spirit-filled church and the pastor greeted me with open arms. He began to counsel me as a new believer, but rather than help me become independent, and find a way to take care of myself and my daughter, he advised me to marry the father of my child whom I had been living with, in order to make things "right with God."

I look back on this with great disdain. I was so excited and overwhelmed with God's love in my life, I would have done anything to please Him. Unfortunately I did not love the father of my child, and actually wanted out of the relationship but did not know how to go about it. I was uneducated, in debt, and desperate. Still, this pastor became my friend and mentor, and I trusted that he knew what God wanted for me.

So I married a man I did not love, and believed God would create love in my heart where there was none. It really did not matter to me because I was so caught up in the church. I was there every time the doors opened. I volunteered, and eventually was hired on in administration. I felt led into the ministry, and attended ministerial training through the church's program. I became an associate pastor after one year of being "saved." The Pastor favored me, and I soaked up every opportunity to learn. He valued the fact that I had not grown up in church. To him I was a "clean slate," and he taught me everything he knew about God and ministry. My husband, however, was not as passionate about serving God. Although he began attending church, he clearly did not possess the passion or ability to lead others as I did. This caused problems in our marriage. I was a preacher and a teacher, and the church was my whole world. I lived and breathed for the church.

Then one day it happened. After two years of being told I was a great minister, I began to question the discernment of my pastor. I wondered if he really understood me and I began to doubt his ability to guide me further in my relationship with God. After all, he had led me into an unfulfilling marriage to someone I did love. My marriage was in shambles. Despite marital counseling, my husband had continued to verbally abuse me, openly shame me and flirt with other women. I felt so lonely, even when he was around. As I inwardly questioned my marriage and my pastor's ability to lead, I put on a display of being a strong leader with no problems. Even when I separated from my husband, the church was unaware. I nurtured, loved, and helped so many of them.

That is why I was shocked at how quickly they all turned on me.

As my husband began to openly cheat on me, the church ignored his unfaithfulness. It was only when I made friends with the music minister, Tim, who was in the final stages of divorce that they stood up and took notice. Gossip permeated the congregation and I began to experience rejection in such a way that I became depressed and vulnerable. When I filed for divorce, I was labeled a whore. More than one person reminded me that God hates divorce. Some told me that divorce was an unpardonable sin. No one talked to me about my marriage, no one advised me, or helped me deal with the feelings I was experiencing. On top of it all, I no longer heard from God. He too became silent, and I felt utterly alone.

I eventually got a divorce, and Tim and I began to date. Admittedly I was emotionally unstable. I had experienced being gossiped about by people that I loved. I was ostracized by my co-pastors, and was deeply depressed when I began to see Tim. We decided to get married three months after my divorce was finalized. When we refused to listen to the Pastor's advice to wait, we were asked to leave the church. The church is quick to shoot its wounded.

CHURCH HOPPING

For months my new husband and I did not attend church at all. We were forced to find secular jobs, which was difficult for us. He had been a minister for twelve years; I had been one for three. Our whole world had turned upside down. We prayed and believed God would not forsake us. So we decided to find another church. But there were none that seemed a good fit for us.

The first church we tried was a non-denominational church. This church was a well-oiled machine! It was all-inclusive: They had something for everyone, and many ways to get connected. We attended for a while and were blessed in many ways. But as time went on we realized the church leaders did not see us as leaders, and there were no opportunities for us to truly get involved. We grew weary of sitting in the pews every Sunday. We didn't want to be entertained; we wanted to be involved. We also began to see how the Pastors were treated like gods in this church. The congregation literally idolized them. It was almost scary, so we left.

The second church we tried was another from the same denomination in which we had worked. We were accepted with open arms, and Tim was asked to lead worship. The church was very small, and the Pastor and his wife were both morbidly obese people who lacked the ability to evangelize the community and build their dying church. They had many meals together as a church, but the congregation lacked life. There were no young people, and once again we grew weary. As loving as they were (and still are) we could not engage them to do more, and could not see ourselves rearranging chairs on a ship that's sinking. So we left this church as well.

After two years of disappointments, we returned to our original church, the one that had asked us to leave. In order to attend there, we were asked to repent of our wrongdoing before the entire congregation. We were so desperate for church fellowship; we did what was asked of us. Yet though we went through a restoration process, the church never respected us again. We bared our souls in front of them, blubbering with repentance and humility, yet they never fully accepted us back into church. We were extremely lonely and no one would befriend us. When the pastor asked us to help another pastor in town who needed a music minister, we went gladly.

A young pastor and his older wife, who were taking over a church within the district, led this church. We arranged a meeting with them, and were impressed by their plans for the church. They were attractive, charismatic, and we all seemed to get along. Tim and I were excited about the opportunity, and we began to help them build their church. However, it wasn't long before we noticed that the pastor's wife controlled her husband.

She frequently corrected and instructed her husband in front of church members. She was demanding, domineering, and quite obviously running the show. She was so assertive I began to feel uncomfortable around her. Rather than allow those feelings to continue, I decided to talk to her. That was a big mistake. She and I sat in her office and had what I felt was a pleasant conversation. I shared my concerns and asked her questions. I thought we had a good talk.

Two days later, members of the church council accused me of attacking the pastor's wife. She lied to them and lied to her husband about our conversation, and made up things I never said. I was floored. She began to openly ignore me. She would walk into a room where I was speaking to someone, and she would speak to them and ignore me. She kept up with this behavior until I just stopped going to church. The ladies in the church also ignored me, and I was treated as though I had done something wrong. My husband and I invited the pastor and his wife to lunch and we talked about it. During our conversation she threatened me with physical violence. That was enough for us.

Battered and bruised, we returned to our home church where we still felt condemned and judged by the congregation. However, it wasn't long before our pastor retired and the church decided to hire the young pastor and his domineering wife from the other church in town. We had just escaped from their craziness, and they followed us back to our home church. In an effort to remain in our church, I attempted to mend the relationship with the pastor's wife by apologizing to her. She accepted my apology, but we never had a good relationship.

About this time, a disgruntled associate pastor approached us. He was going to join another church whose pastor was about to retire and wanted us to join him.

Yet after we joined this other church, the elderly pastor who was supposed to retire decided not to retire after all. He was so excited about us being there and the growth he was experiencing that he decided to keep leading his congregation. This infuriated the associate pastor who had come there thinking he was going to lead, and so he decided to leave and start his own church. He offered us associate positions, and since Tim and I really had no emotional investment in the church, we followed him once more.

In this new church plant, Tim and I were so excited about the possibilities of evangelism and being able to minister and serve God once again in this capacity. But once the church began to experience some growth, we realized the pastor wanted nothing more than to be in control. We realized that he had never been content to be an associate pastor because he was prideful and arrogant. As others joined, he began to distance himself from us. Over time, he became a very unloving pastor.

As his church began to dwindle in numbers, it became apparent to me why he had never successfully established a church before; he was prideful and unloving. He seemed to dislike everyone he met, and was involved in gossip. As the gossip reached its head, I felt deep compassion toward those in the church he had decided he didn't like anymore.

MINISTRY BY EXAMPLE

I left that church over a month ago, and really don't know if I will ever return to church again. Where can I go and worship God without all the drama and rejection of narcissistic so-called Christians who look down their self-righteous noses at a hurting world while attacking one another?

Right now I am just trying to figure out what the church is. My husband has not given up and still ministers, but I minister by example. I love God and want to help others; I just don't know if religion is the same thing as the love of Christ being lived out through me and toward others.

CHAPTER 17
MY SEARCH FOR A FAMILY

By Kellen Freeman

For the past few years, I attended seminary working toward a Master's degree in Biblical Studies. Because it is a United Methodist (UM) seminary, I had friends who were born and raised in the United Methodist church and were, in turn, going to be UM pastors. They never once left the UM tradition, and they never wanted to. My story is different. Though it begins much the same way, it took longer for me to find my place.

LOOKING FOR CHURCH

I grew up in a small town United Methodist church. Calvary United Methodist Church had between 60 and 80 people show up for Sunday services, and only 40 in the summer when half the people went camping. We were a traditional church. Even when we had a younger pastor who encouraged my friends and me to play drums and electric guitars in the sanctuary, the setting remained the traditional liturgy of a UM church. In addition, visits to large-scale youth events such as "Acquire the Fire" instilled in me a desire for a church service focused on the guitar rather than the organ. I knew that if given the chance, I would change where I went to church. I would leave the stuffy world of the United Methodist church for the vibrant world of modern worship.

Eventually that opportunity arose. After leaving home for college I started attending a decent-sized Christian and Missionary Alliance church. I loved the loud music, lack of responsive prayers, and that the songs were sung from projectors instead of books. It was a breath of fresh air for me. I no longer dreaded waking up on Sundays and going to a place of worship I didn't enjoy. Instead, I found myself looking forward to going to church on Sundays with my friends from our campus ministry.

A year later, during my sophomore year of college, I met a girl in the dining hall of campus who would eventually become my wife. Because I wanted to spend time with her, I left the church I was in and moved to the church she was attending. It met in a living room. It was a new church plant that wanted to reach out to college students, so they rented a house right beside campus. Here I spent the next three years of my church life. I lived in the house for the last two of them, helping to pay the rent so we would have somewhere to have meetings and services. I was greatly involved with the work going on there, leading Friday night planning meetings and playing guitar on Sundays. I loved having a purpose and something to do, and I also loved the idea that we were doing church like the apostles did: We met in houses and lived together. At the time, I believed this was the best way of doing church. But eventually we moved on because even this amazing church had lost the luster it once had.

After I graduated from college, I moved to Ohio for seminary. Because I had a big leadership role in the last church plant I was in, I sought out another church plant to work with. But after a short time with them, I stopped going. They were established and didn't need my help. I spent the rest of my first semester in seminary not attending church at all, despite the fact that my school was designed to train pastors.

With only one semester left to live in Columbus before getting married and moving out of the area, I decided to try the church I found online before I even moved to Ohio. It was a church that was founded from a large church-planting network. I figured I would give it a try. They leaned more toward the conservative, but not quite fundamental side, while my beliefs pointed more in the opposite direction. But I didn't care. Even though I didn't agree with everything they said, it helped me to better understand my own beliefs. The church had an art collective that embraced my skills as a former art major. The music was loud and the teaching was relevant. It was my dream church at the time. I could connect here. But before I could truly get involved, I had to move and was not able to return to that church again.

After my wife and I got married, we began looking for a church. Because it was so different from anything else we had tried before, we went to a mega-church down the road. The teaching was good, the music was loud, but it was hard to connect with people. Being full-time students during the week, we were limited to only small groups on the weekend, and those didn't really fit with our interests. We then found ourselves hopping from one church to another. We tried an Assemblies of God, a United Brethren, a Lutheran, an independent, and more. We visited once, twice if we were lucky. Nothing seemed to match what we were looking for. Eventually we gave up. For almost four months, our Sunday mornings were spent watching DIY Network and doing homework.

When 2012 hit, we had been living in our small city for a year and a half and the only person who knew our names was our insurance agent. We decided to make it a goal for the year to find a church and get involved. We didn't want to just attend, but we wanted to get to know people.

We decided to attend the United Methodist church in town to see what it was like. It was more traditional than my home church, which at first made me cringe. I wasn't sure if I wanted to return back to that style. However, after the service, the pastor cornered us before we could escape and asked who we were. She introduced us to someone around our age that lives one town over. We spoke for a little while and then went on our way. It was a glimpse of the interaction I had desired. But that initial interaction seemed to fade as time went on. The last week we were there we heard of another local United Methodist church that had just moved out of the planting phase, and we decided to check it out.

The environment was what we were looking for, and the pastor and his wife made an effort to talk to us. He even asked if I could meet with him after he found out I went to seminary, and the entire group feels friendly. It's still too early to know if this is where we'll fit for the next few years, or how we can be involved, but it feels like we can find a home here, and that's what we're looking for. We know we won't stay in this city forever, and when the time comes to leave, we'll hopefully leave this church as members of a family, not as anonymous visitors.

IT IS FAMILY THAT MAKES A CHURCH

What I've learned over the past few years is that what I really want from a church is community. I want to be a part of a family. When our parents and grandparents live three to seven hours from us, it gets lonely just the two of us. My pap calls me on a weekly basis and lets me know what is going on with my home church. It makes me miss the friends and family I had back home. I missed the church I grew up in. But I was locked a state away for school and couldn't return there if I wanted to unless I dropped out of school and broke my lease. It made me realize I could care less about whether the music is a guitar or an organ, the songs are sung from a projector or a book, or the church meets in a house or an auditorium. I am looking for a family. Someone who knows my struggles, and me cares about who I am, and looks for ways to learn from me while teaching me as well. If I can find that, I can find a church anywhere.

CHAPTER 18
URBAN MISSIONARIES

By Eric Hatfield

In almost 50 years as a Christian, I have been involved in six churches and several independent groups. In every case, we have changed churches for clear, but different reasons. In the process we have learned a lot.

GROWING UP PRESBYTERIAN

Although my parents were not believers, they sent my brothers and me to Sunday school, and encouraged us to go to the youth group and attend church. I don't know why they chose the local Presbyterian Church, but I gained a lot of Bible knowledge in Sunday school, and although I first joined the youth group for social reasons, I learned a lot there as well.

It was a strongly evangelical youth group, with a mildly Reformed basis, and so the teaching was systematic and logical. In this youth group I was challenged to commit myself to faith in Jesus. Around 17, in my first year of studying engineering at the university, I placed my faith in Jesus and began a life of exploration and challenge.

Initially, I accepted the teachings I was given, but I couldn't help feeling something was lacking. Three key areas of faith challenged me, and have continued to challenge me ever since.

First, I had a strong interest in apologetics. I wanted to know that Christianity was true, and I wanted to be able to argue effectively with critics. So I read C. S. Lewis and other apologetic books. Second, I wondered why Jesus' public ministry looked so different than Twentieth century evangelists like Billy Graham, so I began to read biblical scholars to anchor my faith in the reality of the historical Jesus, something that is still important to me. Finally, I began to question the systematic theology I had been taught in this Presbyterian Church.

A DIFFERENT SORT OF PRESBYTERIAN

When we got married in our early 20s, my wife and I were invited to move to another Presbyterian Church to help lead teenagers in the Sunday school. We didn't know to pray about these things then, but we made the move away from our friends and our comfort zone into this new congregation. Before long we were leading the youth group, superintending a Sunday School with over one hundred children, and beginning a number of adult Bible study groups (none had existed before). During this period I also completed a Bachelor of Divinity degree by private study, doing all the work in my spare time.

But this was a more liberal Presbyterian Church than the previous one, and we were challenged to think through whether the evangelical-reformed faith we had been taught was actually true.

We were studying the Bible with the youth group, and reading books from the burgeoning Charismatic and Simple church movements. The book of Acts particularly challenged me. I couldn't help concluding that the early Christians lived more simply than modern western Christians did, their churches were more organic, their faith was stronger, their experience of God was deeper and their mission was carried out more effectively. Since this did not match our modern experience, we were obviously missing something.

We tried to explore these ideas within our church, especially in our youth work, inviting the small group of teens to our house twice a month to interact with our young children, share a meal, listen to music, study the Bible, and share our lives.

I was an elder by then — a lifelong position in the Presbyterian Church — but I came to believe that we were doing church all wrong. When the other elders didn't see things the same way I did, I resigned as an elder and as a member of the church—not out of pique, but out of honesty. If I no longer believed what I had affirmed to become a member and elder, I felt I should resign.

Even though I was no longer an elder or a member, I intended to stay in the church and continue with the other ministries we had taken on, but the church decided otherwise, and told me that I was no longer allowed to teach or lead. Nevertheless, we stayed for a year, with my wife leading Sunday school on her own, before we finally left.

This was a difficult time for both of us, with occasional anger and tears, and a lot of confusion. We met with several groups of elders and ministers from the parish and outside to try to resolve matters. But like Luther, I could "do no other" and the church was unable to change its stance. We realized more than ever before that sometimes Christians could hurt each other deeply, especially when church rules are interpreted pedantically. For a decade afterwards I couldn't return to that suburb without going over the events in my mind. However, I am pleased to say that we were invited to a church reunion many years later, and there was no ill will on either side.

NOT EXACTLY THE WILDERNESS

It was more than nine months before we found another church. We wanted our three young children to understand that meeting together with Christians was important to us and we didn't want them to miss out on regular teaching, so we started a family Sunday school in our home. There were a number of similarly aged children on our street, and they spent a lot of time over at our house. They asked if they could attend also, and so for about 18 months we had an informal Sunday club in our living room with about a dozen children aged between ages four and ten. We saw this as an example of God working things out for good.

During this time I tried out a number of new churches, mostly Congregational (because of my interest in a less hierarchical church) and Pentecostal (because of my ongoing interest in deepening my spirituality). I learnt a lot from these churches, but none of them seemed to be right, and our next step was more pragmatic.

THE BAPTISTS AND BAPTISM

A friend invited us to their Baptist church, and since we wanted to give our young children the opportunity to mix with other children in a more formal Sunday school, we went along. It was a good church, and after a while the youth leaders asked me to join them in leading the large youth group.

I accepted this opportunity enthusiastically, but was then informed that I couldn't continue in this role unless I was baptized as a believer. I had already been baptized as an infant and so declined being re-baptized. I felt that a pragmatic baptism of this sort had no integrity. And so, in Bob Dylan's words, we were "On the Street Again."

SPIRITUAL GROWTH WITH THE PENTECOSTALS

A Presbyterian minister friend invited us to join his church, and it seemed the obvious choice. We would have been welcomed and given opportunities to preach and lead. But a friend at work had been converted by attending a new Pentecostal church in the inner city, and we wanted to check this out.

We decided to give each church a one-month trial. At the end of the two months, we both agreed to join with the Pentecostals. Our reasons were different. I felt I needed to balance my more intellectual approach to belief with the more spiritual emphasis of the Pentecostals, while my wife simply had found her feet in the life of the Spirit and wanted more after experiencing the rather dour Presbyterian Church. It was a steep learning curve, and one of the best decisions we ever made.

The Pentecostal church was full of hundreds of new young converts, and in our mid-30s, we were among the more mature. The music was amazing, the people were enthusiastic, and the church was mission-oriented. They prayed and praised like mad, and we often felt a little bewildered at what went on, but we persevered and soaked it all in.

We eventually became leaders in the children's ministry and for a time I was the leader of a home fellowship group. We made many good friends, experienced inner city life (novel for a couple from the suburbs) and learned much. I never accepted all the Pentecostal doctrines, and despite praying for it, never spoke in tongues. But it was the time of greatest spiritual growth for both of us and we'll never forget those dynamic, challenging days.

The biggest lesson we learned there was to pray. Presbyterian prayer seemed to be muted by their belief in the sovereignty of God, but with the Pentecostals, we learned that God doesn't always exercise His sovereignty, and has delegated some of His work to us. If we want Him to be active on our behalf, we need to *ask* Him.

And so my wife and I committed to pray every morning for each other and our children, something we had only previously done sporadically. Soon our praying expanded to include our ministries, our friends and relatives, the people we were involved with, and whatever else seemed important. Since then we haven't made any decision about ministry, church, family life or work without much prayer. We also learned that the two of us have very different gifts and ways of being guided. She is more intuitive and Spirit-led; I am more persuaded by facts and logic. We have both learned to trust most those decisions where we have consensus for quite different reasons.

There came a time when we knew it was time to leave that church, for we felt the "presidential" and autocratic leadership style was contrary to the New Testament. We prayed for almost a year before God made it quite clear to both of us during one Sunday morning service that it was time to leave. The sermon was about Paul moving on from other ministries to make his way to Rome in the later chapters of Acts, and we both felt that God was giving us directions to leave.

NEW LESSONS, NEW DIFFICULTIES

We decided to join a small but growing Uniting church where a relative attended, because it seemed like the church wanted to try out new approaches to ministry in the community. The church was going through several transitions: from traditional to contemporary, from mostly older people to an influx of young families, and constructing a new building at another location because the existing property had been taken over by the expansion of the local hospital.

In this church, I was part of the group that made plans, and we decided to avoid having a building that was used only a few hours per week. Instead we sought community input on how we could serve them via our building. We bought two old factories, set up a day-care center, and invited local community groups such as Alcoholics Anonymous and other "12 step" groups to meet in the center.

And so began a new stage in ministry for us. We ended up leading services, teaching a small but creative Sunday School group, getting involved with the teens (which by then included our own children), and starting to make connections with the community groups that met in our building.

For eight years we ran a Sunday evening "cafe church" for whoever wanted to come, and it was mostly people with addictions, mental illnesses, or those who were homeless and unemployed. We provided a free meal with some teaching via video (such as *The Jesus Movie*), followed by discussion and interviews. Again, we learned a lot, made a lot of mistakes, had some "hairy" experiences, and saw God at work in the lives of people who found it difficult to be part of the average church. A number of these friends who were struggling in life decided to put their trust in Jesus and we came to understand that caring for the marginalized is as much part of the Good News as is personal salvation.

But this time wasn't without its problems. The church was theologically split between the more theologically liberal who preferred a more traditional approach to church, and the evangelical who were thinking outside the box. And so we knew our days were numbered there, and prayed for a whole year before God led us to our next assignment.

BACK TO THE SUBURBS

We were invited to join a friend in planting a new independent church, but despite the attraction of this idea, we decided this wasn't where God was leading us. So we joined a large, middle class, suburban Anglican Church where interesting things were happening with the youth and young adults.

We are still at this church and have been involved with many of the youth. We have also taken up new understandings about social justice by building and growing a "Justice and Mercy" group.

Almost by accident, we also became part of a small house church originally linked to our church but now independent. For eight years we have shared life and mission with this enthusiastic group of young adults while still attending a big church.

This has been a time of consolidation in my faith. Everything I have learned in all the various churches is coming together. I can see the need for better apologetics and a more historically accurate view of Jesus, the importance of prayer, dependence on the Spirit, caring for the marginalized, and the weakness of a church where the priesthood of all believers is subsumed by the professional clergy and spiritual input comes mainly from one limited perspective.

So we continue in our present church, confident that God will show us his next steps for us, and determined to finish our lives in his service. As we look back, we are amazed and grateful to God for the journey he has led us on and the things he has taught us.

All denominations have their strengths and weaknesses, and Christians can benefit by learning from each other. We've learned that it is crucial to depend on God for our security and significance because churches, ministers and fellow Christians sometimes let each other down. Dependence upon anything or anybody other than Jesus could lead to falling away from faith. And we have learned to pray faithfully and trust that God will lead us, even when we have no real certainty.

It still seems to me that we are a long way short of the personal and community faith the early church had, so we keep hoping, searching, and learning. The life of an urban missionary is never boring!

CHAPTER 19
ONE OF THE BIGGEST PROBLEMS WITH CHURCH IS OFTEN THE PASTOR!

By Wayne W. Hobson

My wife and I had a great dilemma regarding church. Five years ago, we moved to Charlotte from Philadelphia with high hopes of finding a church like the one we belonged to in Pennsylvania. We thought that a small church near our new home in North Carolina was the "one." Our expectations were far from being met after attending this non-denominational church for nearly a year.

We first visited the church for about two months before joining. We thought that we did everything right in selecting this fellowship. We prayed about it, we got to know the pastor, and we made sure that they were a Bible believing church. The sermons were compelling and thought provoking, the members were friendly, the pastor was caring and attentive to the members—everything seemed to be just what my wife and I wanted in a church. Yet, we did not know the real dynamics of the church until after we joined.

THE BIBLE STUDY POWER GRAB

After joining, we began attending Bible Study regularly, along with weekly worship services. Another couple joined around the same time that we did. They had pastored a small church in Florida before moving to Charlotte. Frank and Betty were a friendly and loving couple that were easy going, like my wife and I. Unfortunately for them, their new pastor was not so friendly towards them after Frank humbly turned down the pastor's offer to take over the pastoral office so that she could become an "Apostle" and start another church.

The pastor asked Frank and I to teach a Bible Study on occasion and we did so gladly. But one week the pastor became ill and had to be taken to the hospital when she had a flare up of Chromes disease. I called the pastor's assistant several times to find out who would be leading the Bible study, but received no answer. I left a message, asking her to let me know whether anyone was leading the study that week. I heard nothing from the assistant. Since Frank and I had been the only other ones to teach the Bible study, we discussed which one of us would teach that week if needed. I told him that I had tried to reach the Apostle's assistant, but to no avail. He humbly declined and I prepared a short lesson just in case it was necessary.

When I arrived at the Bible study, Frank was already sitting on the front pew, waiting for others to come in. He asked if I had a lesson ready and I took the two-page lesson from my Bible and handed it to him. About five minutes after the Bible study would have normally begun, the elder of the church came in and approached the podium. He announced that the Apostle left instructions for us to pray in small groups instead of having the usual study. Dumbfounded by this announcement, Frank and I looked at each other, wondering what was going on. I was even more astonished when the assistant came in and refused to even look at me.

After the prayer group ended, I made my way over to the assistant. I tried to sound jovial as I asked if she got my phone message. "Oh, I got it, but I've been on the run this week and didn't get a chance to call you back." She quickly looked over in the direction of the elder. That's when I began to suspect that something else was going on.

My suspicions were confirmed the following Sunday morning when the pastor returned to the pulpit. After service, I went to her office to speak to her. She pretended as if she was glad to see me, but I could feel a wave of thick tension in the air. After exchanging pleasantries, she told me that she heard about how I prepared a lesson for the previous Wednesday night. I explained that I had attempted to reach her assistant to find out if anyone was teaching the study. She told me that she had left the elder in charge and she did not have to report her decisions to anyone. "Your pastor's not an idiot! I'm not going to let the church go without leaving someone in charge," she told me.

I let her know that I understood, but since I was now part of the church leadership committee, I was just trying to be helpful because I didn't know who was leading the study. I insisted that I was not implying that she had to explain her decisions; I had just prepared a lesson in case it was needed. I handed her the lesson, which was still in my Bible, so she could read it for herself, to see what I had planned to teach.

Though the conversation ended on a friendly note, I got the impression that my actions were still misunderstood. I talked to my wife about it and she assured me that I did nothing wrong. I later found out that the assistant had called the pastor after getting my message and the two of them decided that I was trying to take over the church. The pastor had called the elder and instructed him to take over the Bible study. I certainly had no intent on "taking over" anybody's church. To the contrary, my wife and I were now thinking of leaving the church altogether.

POWER AND CONTROL

The final straw that led to us leaving that church came when I received a nasty email from the Apostle. Previously, she had asked me to head up the new Sunday school department. I asked her if I could make an announcement in church about the starting date for this class, and she gave her approval. However, the next day she sent me an email accusing me of "having another agenda than that of the church" and stating that I needed "to fall in line and follow orders." I showed the email to my wife, who was astonished. She knew that the Apostle had approved the announcement beforehand. "Is she crazy or just forgetful?" my wife asked. We decided then that it was time to make our exit.

Sunday school classes had ceased years before when an associate minister stole away a large number of members to start his own church. Apparently, she thought that Frank and I had some similar treachery in mind. I can assure you that we had no such thoughts. Frank told me that he too had received a rather unpleasant email from her after the Bible study incident when he tried to defend me after being asked if he knew anything about what happened. "She just doesn't trust anyone after getting burned. She feels that she must control everything so that she won't lose anything else. It's really sad; she ends up running people off by trying to keep them." He was referring to several other people that had joined the church and later left within months of joining. And now my wife and I were leaving too.

JOY AND FELLOWSHIP

After officially leaving the church, my wife and I visited a few churches, but we were not interested in joining anything again at that point. She was even more apprehensive than I was. Soon, our church visits became less frequent. Weeks went by without us even entering a church. We only visited a church when we felt guilty about being away for so long. Even then, it was a formality and not for true worship. We had become turned off by the politics involved with joining another church. "Church shouldn't be so hard," my wife said to me. "You shouldn't have to navigate through so many personalities and cliques just to find a church home."

We were still very gun-shy about attaching ourselves to another fellowship, but finally, after three years in spiritual limbo, we decided that it was time to start seriously looking again. We visited a large Baptist church near downtown Charlotte. The service was nice, the people seemed cordial, and the pastor, an older man in his early seventies, seemed to be seasoned and approachable. After the service, we were invited to the fellowship hall, where they gave us gift bags, and the associate minister asked if we had any prayer requests and then prayed sincerely for our needs. We felt comfortable and went back the next Sunday and the Sunday after that.

After a few months of visiting, my wife and I began praying about committing to this church. Both of us enjoyed going to church again for the first time in years. We felt there was room for us to serve God there and it seemed to be a right fit for us spiritually. I was completely won over when I briefly talked to the associate pastor after service one Sunday. Even though it had been four months since he had prayed for us, he accurately remembered who we were and how he had prayed for us. He even remembered my mother-in-law's name and the health concern that we expressed to four months previously. I was floored! That church has around 1000 members and numerous visitors each week, yet he remembered us! After some prayer and consideration, we joined the church less than a month later.

We are joyful about going to church again. We gladly attend Bible study, worship, and Sunday school regularly. And after the pastor learned of our teaching skills, he appointed my wife and I to head a spiritual gifts class that he wants the entire congregation to go through. Spiritual gifts are something he has wanted the church to grow in and he had been praying for someone to teach a class.

We have not enjoyed being a part of a church this much since our former church in Pennsylvania. We feel like God is using us here.

CHAPTER 20
LOYALTY

By Kimberly Parker

One balmy day in the South Pacific, a navy ship espied smoke coming from one of three huts on an uncharted island. Upon arriving at the shore, they were met by a shipwreck survivor. He said, "I'm so glad you're here! I've been alone on this island for more than five years!"

The captain replied, "If you're all alone on the island why do I see *three* huts?"

The survivor said, "I live in one and go to church in another."

"What about the *third* hut?" asked the captain.

"That's where I *used* to go to church."

Loyalty is defined as carrying strong feelings of commitment, support or faithfulness to an ideal, a thing, a place, or a person. Loyalty is both spoken and unspoken. Although you wouldn't declare allegiance to Crest toothpaste, the fact that you've purchased it regularly for the past 25 years demonstrates unspoken loyalty.

Spoken loyalty is when you take your bright white smile and stand before the congregation at your church, committing to membership and faithful service.

That's exactly what my husband and I did about four years ago. We had moved to a new city and found a new church home. We committed to be a positive, contributing family to that church, to tithe faithfully and to serve wholeheartedly. We did our best to live up to that pledge. Yet, two and a half years later, we revoked our membership.

Was that breaking our loyalty? Some would think so. Some *did* think so. You see God totally digs loyalty. The entire Bible is a love story about His loyalty to the Israelites throughout their unfaithfulness to Him. Knowing that God wants us to honor our commitments, I was at odds with how to proceed when I felt we should leave. How does loyalty fit into church membership? Do you stay at a church you said you would serve—even if they head off in a different direction? In the Bible, there were times God had people stay put and initiate change and times where He had them "go." What were we to do?

Questions plagued me as the feeling that we needed to leave grew. I believe we approached it biblically and I want to share three things that contributed to knowing the best course of action.

BECOME A BEREAN

In my ministry involvement, I met a woman who became my closest friend. We had many things in common, including a hunger to study God's Word and discover creative ways to bring it to life. We co-led a ministry program that offered Bible study to more than 100 women each week.

It was so much fun to work together, developing biblical teaching messages. A passion within each of us was ignited. She discovered a love for teaching and speaking at live women's events; I learned to use my writing gifts for God. We identified a desperate need to encourage and equip others with truth, and did our best to meet that need.

Through our regular contact with women each week we realized many women are not comfortable coming to a Bible study group or, due to life's circumstances, are not able to get out of the house regularly. We also recognized that if this was the case in our town, it was likely the case all across the world.

A vision took shape for us to take our ideas and create online resources, designed to connect believers across the world, while teaching sound biblical truth in a practical, applicable way.

We began recording podcast teaching messages and making them available on iTunes. We also wrote two Bible studies. Our speaking engagements led to our writing a book that was published in August 2010. We immersed ourselves in Scripture every day.

I give you this background to point out that it wasn't until I got serious about studying God's Word that I was able to see in my personal life where I needed to get tougher with my own sin and obedience to God. Then, from that launching pad, God was able to teach me all kinds of lessons. It is also why I was able to discern the growing feelings of discomfort at our church.

In Acts 17 we learn about a group of believers called the Bereans who were of noble character because they received the message from Paul with great eagerness and examined the Scriptures every day to see if what he said was true (Acts 17:11).

Even though Paul himself taught the Bereans, they searched the Scriptures every day. This is an example for every believer. Time and again God tells us to know his Word. Studying Scripture is the only way we will know when something does not line up with it.

Leaving our church began with a "feeling" that something was amiss. A new pastor arrived with a new shift in direction, new teachings he promoted, and new goals he announced. I felt uncomfortable with some of these new directions, but I wouldn't have known what those feelings were about if I wasn't studying Scripture. I also wouldn't have been able to distinguish my own sinful feelings from what I observed around me if I wasn't tough with my own sin.

Without Scripture, my feelings could have turned into deeper levels of dissatisfaction or resentment. It could have been assumed I simply had a different "opinion" than our pastor. It may have led to a disagreement with a brother or sister, possibly even resulting in hurt feelings.

But because I studied the Bible, I knew it was none of those things. Because I sought my own repentance first, I was able to know I had nothing against a brother or sister. We left because the new direction and new declared goals did not line up with Scripture. Period.

We could have easily sat in the pews, Sunday after Sunday, simply listening. We could have assumed the authors our church promoted and the videos shown in the service were reliable without checking into them or asking questions. Many people experience church in that way.

Yet, that is neither the example nor the lesson we are given in Scripture. We must approach everything we do as Bereans.

ASK TOUGH QUESTIONS

When you seek truth in Scripture, you will have questions. You will see things you may not initially understand. You will wonder about the biblical basis for the things you hear and the things you read.

It is important to have a fellowship of believers with whom you can digest and expound on biblical truths. It is important to be able to ask tough questions and search for answers with others who are also in a continual state of repentance and who seek to handle things biblically.

If the tough questions need to be asked of your church leadership, do so respectfully and with a true heart to learn truth (not to be "right"). I noticed our church began to promote speakers and authors whose content was under extreme controversy as straying from the whole truth of God's Word. When leadership was asked about this, we were told there are many good ideas in evangelical Christianity and we shouldn't throw out the whole thing, just because part of what someone teaches might not be fully accurate. This does not line up with Scripture.

Unless we asked, we would not have known.

GIVE GOD ROOM TO SPEAK

My husband and I were not in agreement initially that we should change churches. He, too, felt uncertain about the new messages and materials being promoted, but he wasn't sure leaving was the answer.

We had made some very good, Jesus-loving friends at this church. He had been involved in helping the staff in some practical ways, and he was thankful for how we had been blessed by our friends there.

I certainly considered making a strong push for a family church change. However, the Holy Spirit cautioned me against it. I told God I would respect my husband's decision as head of our home. I shut my own mouth about my concerns and allowed God room to speak to my husband.

I made this commitment knowing that I might not get my way. I had to decide to be okay with allowing my husband to lead. A few weeks later, after church one Sunday, he declared with strong conviction that we needed to find another church.

It would have been easy for me to think I knew best and I could have driven the decision to change churches. But that would not be honoring to my husband. I needed the patience and trust for God to either confirm what I felt or show me where I was wrong.

SO WHAT WAS THE DISCREPANCY?

I shared my process for working through our change before explaining the problem itself, because the process is valuable, no matter what the challenge. In our case, our church took on a new vision with a primary focus to be a seeker-friendly place, where people in the community can come and not feel heavily pressured by a biblical teaching to turn their life over to Christ.

Their declared goal became to *be* Jesus, with less emphasis on *telling* others about him. The overriding question for everything was, "How do we get more people to come to church?"

This isn't necessarily a bad question, but consider the danger when it becomes the *main* question. Being Jesus is, indeed, a part of our call, but telling about him is just as critical.

The consequences will be great if a church operates from the standpoint that people in the community won't come if they are asked outright to turn their lives to Christ. If a church's primary goal is to get people in the doors, strategies to reach this goal affect the decisions made about what to do, what to preach, and who should lead programs. The church begins to look like the community that surrounds it.

This might seem like a good plan because upon arriving at church, the visitor is made to feel comfortable. But there is no staying power to such an approach because if the purpose is just to get people in the door, the purpose is achieved once people arrive. Can lives be changed, bonds broken, and hearts transformed from a place of comfort? Not in my experience.

Sadly, most people in the pews don't even realize what is happening. They may feel something is missing, but can't put a finger on what. People believe they are still on mission for God, but the mission is really about making friends, not making believers. The Parable of the Ten Virgins is a strong warning that many will think they are part of the wedding party because they look the part and are in the right place, but they will find themselves without oil when Jesus returns. I can think of nothing sadder.

WHAT IS LOYALTY?

Loyalty doesn't mean blind allegiance to people. Loyalty doesn't mean avoiding asking tough questions to avoid controversy.

Loyalty means handling a matter with Biblical wisdom guiding your actions. It involves respecting those in leadership and taking your questions and concerns to them to seek truth.

In some cases, the Lord might have you stay put. In other cases, He may ask you to go.

How do you know what to do? Unless you are deep in prayer and connected to Scripture, you won't be able to discern the best course of action. Too often people change churches based solely on a feeling — without knowing the source of the feeling or even if it is a God-honoring feeling.

God will lead us to things for His purposes. In our continued loyalty to Him alone, He will also show us when and if it is time to allow Him to lead us onward, with His rich lessons in our souls.

CHAPTER 21
A REFUGE IN TIMES OF TROUBLE

By Felisa Reed

I "accepted Jesus into my heart" in a tiny Southern Baptist church with stained glass windows. The preacher gave an impassioned speech about sin: how we all had it, were doomed because of it, and we desperately needed Jesus to save us from it. He invited anyone ready to admit to being a hopeless sinner to come down the aisle, kneel, and repeat a prayer to receive salvation. I knew deep in the core of my being that there was evil in my heart, and I was desperate for Jesus to save me from it. I was five years old.

Many people who hear that part of my story assume that the church in question must have been an awful place, full of judgment and condemnation. Nothing could be further from the truth. The forms of our worship were old-fashioned: we sang hymns along with an organ or piano, were baptized in borrowed white robes, and always came in our Sunday best. The love in that small community, however, was anything but stodgy and old-fashioned. The members there cared for one another spiritually, emotionally, and with what practical help they could manage. If someone came in looking out of place — dressed in black leather or with tattoos on his face — they might look over their shoulders during the service, but afterwards, the members there would make him feel truly welcome.

MOUNTAIN CHURCH

When I was eight, my family moved to a new city. We spent several weeks hunting for a church. We encountered one church that seemed to be a frightening cult, but eventually settled on a new church home (I'll call it "Mountain Church," though of course I've changed the name). There were over 500 people in attendance every Sunday, so it looked like a huge crowd to my little eyes. It was non-denominational, evangelical Christian, with an official policy of welcoming everyone. There was no official dress code. There were also donuts every Sunday morning.

I attended Mountain Church until I was 17, but even after nine years, I felt like a stranger. Although officially they wanted to welcome everyone, close observation would reveal that the Mountain Church was rather homogeneous, far more so than the metropolitan area where it was located. There were around 1000 in attendance by the time I left, and nearly all of them were middle class, fair skinned, had no more than three children per family, came to church dressed business casual, watched the same sorts of movies, and followed the same sports teams. They even listened to the same 40 songs. I felt terribly isolated.

I wish to be very clear: I do not think anyone at that church intended to make other people feel unwelcome. They didn't necessarily think, for example, that hard rock was evil; they simply preferred repetitive Christian pop. I remember one friend telling me her mother felt excluded because other members' conversations frequently reminded her of her financial troubles; it probably never occurred to them that conversations about charitable contributions might be difficult for people struggling just to feed their families. The members of Mountain Church made every effort to include anyone who walked through the door, but their own cultural experiences were limited, and they didn't know what to say to those whose experience was different.

For me, the experience of exclusion was subtle. The youth group was populated with members of only one or two of the myriad high school cliques. "Jocks," both male and female, were welcome, and all those who sought to be part of the popular crowd. I had never fit with those sorts. For one thing, I was very intellectual, and anyone who came across as too smart at my high school was in danger of losing popularity. For another thing, I didn't keep track of famous actors, follow any sports, or listen to popular music. I was far more interested in good books, local politics, and meaningful lyrics. When I tried to talk about things I was interested in, someone always changed the subject to topics I knew nothing about.

Of course, this feeling of not belonging is quite common in high school. If it had been limited to small talk before and after meetings, it might not even have mattered. In order to make things relevant, however, youth group discussions constantly tied in to things the popular kids knew about. To me, it was like a foreign language. When we talked about the Bible, I had plenty to contribute; so much so, in fact, that I came across as a know-it-all. My speech was as incomprehensible to the rest of the youth group as theirs was to me. Other teens came for the socialization, and put up with the Bible studies as a means to that end. I came for the Bible study, and was utterly bewildered by the social aspect. I seemed only to alienate my fellow students any time I opened my mouth.

BIBLE COLLEGE CHURCH

I went away to a Christian college on the west coast. I suppose I expected to find many like-minded friends there, but I encountered the same problem I had in high school. Even though the multitudes in heaven come from every tongue, tribe, and nation, most of the multitudes at this college listened to those same 40 Contemporary Christian songs.

I found a church whose college group discussions were intellectually engaging and which taught doctrine mostly consistent with my own beliefs. Yet I still found myself out of place. Everyone there was an extrovert, a morning person, and rarely questioned any point of doctrine.

One day, we played a game called "Have You Ever" for an icebreaker, and someone called out, "I've never spoken in tongues," just as a joke. I stood, alone, evidently the only member of the group who had experienced such a thing. I still remember the stares of this usually open, accepting group, shocked and appalled to learn that I could believe in miraculous gifts of the Holy Spirit occurring in modern America. I'm not even sure whether what had happened to me was "speaking in tongues." I explained this, to fill the painful silence. Yet the fact that I had doubt on a point of doctrine, even one I considered relatively unimportant, seemed to be even more shocking to this group than the idea that I might have reached a different conclusion after thoughtful consideration of the same Bible. After two years at that church, I once again gave up trying to feel at home among my own brothers and sisters in Christ.

I drifted in and out of church for my last three years on the west coast. Then, like so many of my generation, I wound up having to move back in with my mother when I could not find a stable job. I tried, for a little while, to go back to my old non-denominational church, and found that I felt just as disconnected there as I had as a teenager.

REFUGE CHURCH

I re-entered a long struggle with depression. After getting to know me a bit, my therapists, to whom I had been referred by my old church, recommended I try a new church. It was a very small church, and home to a lot of recovering addicts. It was pastored by a man and a woman, equal co-pastors, both married, but not to each other. They told me it was an eclectic community, full of broken people, and that I'd fit right in. Though I felt their speech was hardly complimentary, I knew what they meant, and decided to try it out.

It is an odd place. They have no doctrinal statement at all, as a matter of policy, and their meetings focus on discussion rather than teaching. Anyone can speak in the discussions, and the group listens attentively and sympathetically to everyone, including those with whom they disagree. It is true what those therapists said: it is home to many broken people. It seems to me that every church is made of broken people, though this is hidden in most churches. Here, that brokenness is out in the open. There are recovering addicts in leadership positions. Many members struggle with codependence. There are many who struggle with depression, as I do, and others who live with more severe mental illness. It is a place of brokenness, but because the people there welcome honesty and practice acceptance, it is also a place of healing.

I would not say that I am normal in my current church, but it does not matter, because no one is. There is no normal, so no one feels strange. It is a place of unity in diversity, even in areas of doctrine.

Of course, this diversity can lead to conflict. For example, we have members who practice monogamous homosexuality and consider themselves followers of Christ, and other members who believe homosexuality is sin. Discussions can become heated. At the end of the day, however, everyone usually parts in friendship, because we do not take it upon ourselves to judge and condemn one another. Instead, we look to God to convict people of sin, to each individual to examine his or her own conscience, and to each other to love and support one another through every struggle and triumph. There are still partings of ways from time to time, but we find we can coexist, and need not leave simply because we disagree. Instead, we seek the truth together, and focus on love for each other and for Christ.

I have found my refuge here. Though like-minded teachers do not reinforce my beliefs, my faith still grows stronger, because I am putting it into practice. No one condemns me for my sin, yet they are there to support and correct when I know I need to change.

It is ironic that I found healing in a church with no doctrinal statement, truth in a place where the members constantly disagree about doctrine, and love where I would have expected animosity. I am learning more about sanctification from this group of honest, redeemed sinners than I did among so many who claimed knowledge of the truth.

If I am tempted, however, to abandon my search for truth and conclude that true community cannot exist where doctrine is set and agreed upon in writing, I need only remember those Southern Baptists with their stained-glass windows and warm welcomes who cheered when I, a five-year-old sinner, accepted Jesus into my heart.

CHAPTER 22
LOOKING FOR THE KINGDOM

By Sam Riviera

The stovepipe glowed red from the top of the wood-burning stove to the ceiling. Even though an icy storm was blowing outdoors, Mother ran back and forth between the stove and outdoors, shouting "Chimney fire! I'm going to burn down Annie's house! The pipe is red where it comes out of the roof and flames are shooting out of it at least ten feet!"

Annie was elderly and lived alone. She almost never cleaned her old house. Instead of sweeping the floor, she spread out each day's newspaper on the old, tired, filthy linoleum. She often forgot to wipe the mud off her shoes after working in her garden. By the time the cold northwest winds blew in the first storms of the winter, Annie's layers of newspapers on the floor had grown quite deep and quite filthy.

In the summer, Mother and I helped Annie pick strawberries in her garden. Annie was too proud to accept "charity," so we took her fishing so she would have protein to eat. We took her fishing only in warm weather so we could roll down the car windows for some fresh air. Annie rarely bathed.

The Saturday morning of the big chimney fire Mother and I had shown up at Annie's house armed with buckets, brushes, and other cleaning supplies.

"Annie, you just sit down and relax while we help you tidy up a little," announced Mother.

The first order of the day was picking up six months of newspapers off the floor. Mother decided to burn them in Annie's pot-bellied wood-burning stove. That was a big mistake.

"Do you have insurance on this house, Annie?" Mother sobbed as she ran in the door.

"No. But don't worry about it. Ralph and I had a chimney fire twenty years ago and the house didn't burn down." Annie, sitting in her old rocking chair, smiled and continued to rock, seemingly without a care in the world.

"That pipe's red-hot and flames are shooting out the chimney!" Mother shouted as she once again ran out into the snow and sleet.

Annie continued to rock in her chair and Mother continued to run back and forth between the potbellied stove and the yard to check the roof. Eventually the chimney fire burned itself out and the stovepipe no longer glowed red.

"See, I told you the house wouldn't burn down," Annie told us. "Now the soot and tar is all burned out of the stovepipe and at my age I should never have to worry about another chimney fire."

I spent the rest of the morning and half the afternoon on my hands and knees scrubbing the floor with a large brush and buckets of soapy water while my mother washed windows, wiped months of accumulation of dust off the furniture and cleaned the bathroom.

As we drove home late that afternoon, allowing just enough time to get supper ready by the time my father got home from work, I asked my mother, "Why do we have to clean old people's houses? They don't even pay us anything."

"Because they don't have anyone else to help them and they're not able to do it themselves," replied my mother.

In addition to helping Annie, we helped Mildred and her elderly brother Robert, Clyde, Tom, and an assortment of other elderly people who lived alone. I especially disliked helping clean Tom's and Clyde's homes, because they smelled of years of stale cigar smoke and urine.

As a boy, I didn't understand why my mother did such things. I much preferred the activities at my hometown church.

CHURCH ACTIVITIES

Hiking into a snowy woods in early December to cut a wild evergreen, dragging it back home and loading it in the trunk of the car, then taking it to our little white clapboard-sided church with the high steeple that enclosed the bell I rang each Sunday was more to my liking.

That little church was where I heard about Jesus. That little church was where I was baptized when I was twelve, a very significant moment for me wherein I confirmed that I was Christ's and he was mine.

When that little church experienced dramatic decline in my teen years, I became the church janitor, the children's Sunday School teacher, the one who turned on the church furnace every Saturday evening in the winter, the Sunday morning bell ringer, the one who cut and decorated the church Christmas tree and placed pine boughs and candles in each window, readying the church for the arrival of the Christ child.

The crisis that precipitated my high level of involvement in church eventually passed (today that little church is the largest church in the community), but my level of church involvement continued. My wife, who also grew up in church, joined me in extreme church involvement.

EXTREME CHURCH INVOLVEMENT

We soon had no time to help old people or clean their houses. We were part of countless church committees, led Bible studies, cooked hundreds of church dinners and banquets, taught Sunday school classes, led meetings, and did dozens of other jobs in the churches of which we were a part.

We were part of the team that greeted people as they came to church. Eventually we headed that team. We arrived early and stood near the door until the sermon began. I usually stayed outside, on the edge of the patio in front of the doors and greeted people as they arrived.

We knew everyone who attended the church, even those who had attended just one time. We remembered their names. We greeted them by name when we ran into them at the grocery store and the hardware store. They waved at us and stopped to talk to us each evening as we walked our dog through the streets of the community. They talked to me on the church patio and told me their problems and their joys. They confided in me about their troubled marriages, lost jobs, wayward children, and even their anger toward the church. When the pastor needed to know something about someone, he called us first.

That was all years ago. I have left that church and though I am no longer involved in such activities, I have learned new ways to serve others in the Kingdom of God.

SERVING IN THE KINGDOM

On a recent Sunday morning a few friends and I were picking up trash in the streets that surrounded a church building in an inner city neighborhood in the city where we live. As church folk parked in the streets and headed toward their church building, they walked in a wide arc around my little group and me. They assumed, as we later learned, that we were doing some sort of community service to pay for some crime they imagined we had committed. After all, why else would anyone pick up trash along streets in an inner-city neighborhood?

The church folk settled into their pews and my little group split up. Each of us took one street. My street passed directly in front of the church. A few minutes later I found myself standing across the street from the open front doors of the church. I could hear singing and shouting coming from within. I noticed that the church property was immaculate. The grass was green. No trash littered the church lawn and sidewalk, though on either side of the church and on my side of the street, litter was strewn everywhere.

As the praise songs flowed out of the open doors of the church and I picked up trash, a lady who lived next to the church approached me.

"Who are you and why are you picking up the trash in our street?" she asked.

"We're Jesus' followers and we're trying to show some love to the neighborhood."

"Are you part of that church?" she asked, pointing to the church with the open doors.

"No," I replied. "We don't know anything about those folks."

"They don't like us. They call the cops on us all the time. My boy threw a candy wrapper on their lawn and they called the cops. No one who lives around here has ever stepped foot in that place and we never will."

My new friend and I talked about the neighborhood, her family, and Jesus. She cried. We hugged. As she departed another neighborhood lady approached me with a similar story and similar questions, followed by a third lady when the second lady departed.

Later, as I reflected on these conversations, I asked myself "Where is the Kingdom that Jesus introduced?"

WHERE IS THE KINGDOM?

Are Jesus and the Kingdom present in the buildings that bear the word "church"? Is the Kingdom active when people meet in those buildings across the city and across the nation in which we live? It is possible. I have met with followers of Jesus and felt his presence at such places in years gone by. I assume that Jesus continues to meet with his followers as they gather in his name, wherever that may be.

However, I do know what living in the Kingdom of God looks like for me as I follow Jesus today.

A few weeks ago, after spending a couple of days doing laundry (clothes from our friend's failed thrift store—my wife and I called it "the rag picker's shop"), I thought about what are the best ways to serve the Kingdom. For many years, we allowed the Institutional Church to tell us what serving God and living in the Kingdom looks like. They may teach some good ideas, but their way is not the only way to serve in the Kingdom. For us, serving in the Kingdom looks like taking whatever we have in our hands, and using it to love and help those whom God places in our path.

We are living in the Kingdom when we spend time with Angela the "rag picker" at her shop and with her customers, washing the clothes, hanging them on the clothesline so they would smell fresh, then giving the clean clothes to people who need them that very night to keep warm and dry out on street.

The Kingdom looks like talking to the people on the street and listening to their stories. The Kingdom looks like hugging those who want to be hugged. The Kingdom looks like giving a bottle of water to the thirsty. The Kingdom looks like talking to the guy with staples in his head from the top of his head to his chin (knife fight or tree branch — whichever version of the story you like) when everyone else avoids him.

The Kingdom looks like picking up garbage off the streets of an inner city neighborhood and talking to the people who walk past. The Kingdom looks like hugging a biker on his Hog in the middle of the street in the inner city. The Kingdom looks like talking to people and answering their questions about churches, God, and the Bible as the church folk, dressed in their Sunday finest, and clutching their Bibles to their breasts, give us a wide berth on their way to worship God.

The Kingdom looks like picking up used needles on the street, as the neighbors peer from behind their curtains. In a few minutes, some of them come out of their doors and ask who we are and why we do what they are afraid to do. The Kingdom looks like answering their questions with, "We're followers of Jesus and wanted to do something nice for the neighborhood," and seeing their smiles in response.

The Kingdom looks like spending time with our neighbors, hearing their stories, and getting to know them. It looks like making chili, buying lots of candy and cider, setting up a fire pit on the driveway and inviting the neighborhood to gather on Halloween around a warm fire with a warm bowl of chili as they get to know each other.

The Kingdom looks like not doing what we do so we can "invite people to church." We are the church, the church in the neighborhood, the church with a bottle of water, the church with a warm coat and a tarp. We are the church that will listen to your story, the church that will give you a hot cup of soup, the church that will wrap its arms around you when you need it.

Now I understand why my mother and I helped old people. I understand why we sat and listened to their stories. I understand why we cleaned up their dirty houses. We were the church; we are the church, the Kingdom of God at work.

CHAPTER 23
A COLLECTIVE YES

By Cara Sexton

"It's too small. I don't want fifteen phone calls and four elders coming to the door if I don't show up one Sunday, you know? I don't want to feel like I have to deliver a casserole every time a random old lady has a hip replacement."

My husband rolled his eyes while continuing to plead his own case. "Fine, but I don't want to be just a number in a building the size of a shopping mall. I don't want to have to go through sixteen committees and an entrance exam just to be able to serve in the church."

This argument had been going on for a decade and yet we'd never found a church that felt like home. One had great worship but we couldn't seem to get plugged in. Another had sermons that rocked us to the core, but the worship felt staged and we were lost in the crowd. We knew everyone at this church and nobody at that one. We served too little at this church, too much at that one.

Too country. Too casual. Friendly, but not deep enough. Too much anecdote, not enough Scripture. Too much Scripture, not enough explanation. Too much finger-wagging, not enough Jesus. Too traditional. Too inclusive. Bad child care. No friends. No emphasis on missions. Not enough community involvement. Too political. Too crowded. Too early. Too boring. Too big. Too small. Too far to drive.

WHY WAS IT SO DIFFICULT?

When it comes to life in general, we are notoriously laid back people. We are generally easy to please. When purchasing a home, we bought the first house we looked at. We are not picky or particular and our expectations didn't seem terribly unrealistic. So why had this church thing been so difficult? We just wanted to love and learn about Jesus.

Despite our multiple attempts at finding a church community to call home, we didn't exactly spend our weekends church hopping. We'd spent six months or longer attending every church we'd tried, but each stint only raised the bar by shedding light on the strengths of one and the weaknesses of another. We often joked about piecing together a church by cutting and pasting various aspects from each of the churches we'd been a part of.

Adding to the struggle were our differences in preference and upbringing. I met Jesus as a teenager in a large community church with a rockin' youth group, and I wanted my kids to have the same experience. My husband had a traditional and reverent spiritual upbringing; with tight community ties and a deep desire to get his hands dirty. I'm an introvert; he's an extrovert. I wanted to get lost in the crowd while he wanted to shake hands with the entire congregation every Sunday.

We grew weary of searching and our laundry list of complaints grew larger. Despite our difficulties in church-seeking, we'd worked together in full-time ministry as house parents at a Christian children's home, quickly discovering that the institution of Christian ministry was as flawed as the Church under all its human influence. We longed to make a difference for Christ and spent our days pouring into the lives of others. All we wanted was to find a church that could refill our emptied vessels and revive our weary spirit. Was that so much to ask?

As it turns out, it was.

Defeated, we decided to spend a few Sundays sleeping in to give the whole church thing a break. A few weeks turned into a few months, and our laziness battled our longing to return to weekly fellowship. It took a complete church hiatus for us to face the somber reality: We wouldn't find the church we were looking for. Not in this county, not in this country, not in this world, not in this lifetime.

Putting distance between the church community and ourselves gave us a fresh perspective in our hunt for a church home. Humbled, we realized our search for a church needed to be more like looking for a job than shopping for a house. After all, we are not called to *go* to church; we are called to *be* the Church. What happened within the walls on Sunday morning was not nearly as important to the cause of Christ as what happened outside those walls the rest of the week.

THE CHURCH WE'D BEEN LOOKING FOR

We'd been looking for a church to do what only Jesus could. The church could not fill us or restore us. We wanted a church that would give us something, but it turned out *we* were the problem. Collectively speaking, *people* are what is wrong and what is right about the Church. We are the flawed and hurting, imperfect and striving, saved-by-grace Bride of Christ. We are too small and too big. Too busy and too sinful. Too inclusive and too loud. Too selfish and too distant. We are, all at once, the shining jewel of Scripture and the hypocritical brick wall standing between our neighbors and salvation.

It didn't matter much which sanctuary we planted our bodies in, what mattered was the condition of our hearts. And as it turns out, church was not a spectator sport. It was a living, breathing organism, a work in progress, and a blemished vessel to reflect the redemption of a perfect Savior. Church is a bit of a purgatory — where a dimension of blameless perfection meets the world of the wretched, where sick souls are soothed, where barren lives bear fruit, where we live and learn and succeed and fail and fall at the feet of the One who has overcome it all on our behalf.

We *are* the Church, and what is wrong with the institution is what is wrong with our souls, but what is redeeming about the Church is what will eventually overcome the flaw of humanity, the fall of mankind. The Church is not perfect, but the Savior is, and (spoiler alert!), He wins. He wins over greed, over sin, over doubt. He wins over fear, over death, over hypocrisy.

The Church is just a collective *yes*, a mutual shuffling of sorry souls to the fountain of grace. It is a kiln where we are fired and made brick, piled together to form a path that leads our communities and neighbors, our enemies and friends along Calvary's road to the foot of the cross, a winding trail of broken brick, bringing others from darkness into the light of Christ.

We couldn't find church in a building until we found it in within ourselves. We couldn't pulse with the lifeblood of the body until we stitched our feet to it, transfused our souls, and breathed the sweet yet temporal breath of this being called Church.

SECTION 3
REFORMING CHURCH

I believe that the church is going through seismic changes today, which will not be fully seen or understood for several hundred years. The church of 200 years from now will look nothing like the church of 200 years ago, or even the church of today. In a sense, today is the Second Reformation.

Therefore, all of us who seek to be part of the way church is changing may view ourselves as Reformers. And we *are* reforming the church; or at least trying.

I consider myself as one of these reformers, and as a reader of this book, you should too. We are all seeking to bring the vision of Jesus Christ for this world into reality by living according to his teachings, and by loving others we come into contact with each day. Such a task must be renewed with every generation. We must not rest upon the laurels of the past, but in every age must strive for God's Kingdom to come and his will to be done on earth as it is in heaven.

Though I have attended and pastored lots of local churches and through I no longer attend church in a building, I believe I am more active in church today than ever before. Like so many others, I am hoping, praying, and working for the church to change into what God wants so that we can better follow Jesus into the world.

Below are three areas I am focusing on in my own life.

First, I desire that my primary form of church is my personal involvement with those in life whom God has placed around me. As a follower of Jesus, I want to show tangible love to my family, my neighbors, my coworkers, and the random strangers

I meet every day. Learning how to do this is a big struggle for me, but two people who have helped me most in this are my wife, Wendy, and my friend, Sam Riviera (who contributed a chapter for this book). The two of them are masters at showing love to others. I am thankful that God has placed Wendy and Sam in my life so that I can follow them as they follow Jesus. They have shown me that loving others in tangible ways causes us to be the hands and voice of Jesus to them. When we live this way, we *are* the church to the people around us. It is as Sam likes to say: When we are the church, it looks so much like Jesus.

Second, as we come alongside people in their joys and trials and seek to love and serve them in tangible ways, Wendy and I dream of joining or starting some sort of Christian community. It wouldn't be a church. From the outside, it would probably look more like a group of friends who hang out together. But from the inside, we would know that we were much more. Our focus and goal would be to learn about Jesus and take practical steps toward advancing the rule and reign of God in our town and in our neighborhoods. Right now, we are only in the dreaming stage, but we believe that as God brings clarity to our vision and brings more people into our lives with similar dreams, such a community will organically form and will help others reimagine what "church" can look like outside of a building.

Finally, as a chaplain in a prison, I participate in a form of church that is institutional to the extreme. Everything in a prison is guided by rules, schedules, and policies. This is a challenge for me because of the values and beliefs I have about church. But at the same time, it has been exciting for me to watch the men I work with come to an understanding of the freedom and flexibility that we have as followers of Jesus. It is thrilling to lead them in trying creative approaches to ministry and new ways of loving others. Recently, I was able to show one of the Bible Study groups that it was okay to cancel their Bible study every other week so that they could go put into practice what they learned in Bible study the previous week. Imagine if churches around the country did such a thing?

Exciting things are happening in Christianity, and when creative ideas meet courageous Christians, a church that exists only in our dreams will begin to emerge.

Below are some stories from people who are taking creative steps in their own church. The stories that follow are from people who have experienced the pain and hardship of attending a church, but rather than leave church or switch churches, have decided to stick around and love and forgive from within. These are the courageous stories from people who seek to reform the church from within the four walls.

CHAPTER SUMMARIES

Alan Brisco hopes and dreams for what millions of others long for: a community of people who love and serve one another in tangible ways as they live life with one another in their towns and neighborhoods. He shares five things he is looking for in such a community.

After Kris Camealy grew frustrated at the lack of volunteers and involvement in her church, she began to fantasize about attending a newer and more active church. But then she remembered Paul's instruction that love is the key to functioning as the church, and she decided to start showing love to her church by serving and praying for the people in it. Before long, she found that she didn't need a new church; she needed a new heart for her church home.

Beginning with the story of Jonathan Edwards and the challenges he faced in his own church, Daniel Darling reminds us that the church is indispensable for following Jesus into the world, engaging others with the gospel, and growing into maturity in our walk with God. He uses biblical and theological insights to encourage people to remain engaged with the church, no matter what failures and weaknesses it might have.

Melody Harrison Hanson desires to be in a church that is fully egalitarian. The church she attends has no female pastors or elders, and limits women from using all of their spiritual gifts. This frustrates Melody, but she stays in her church in the hope that she can be a catalyst for change, and can lead the church to begin the conversation about women's role in ministry.

After Dan King became a Christian, he set out to study Scripture and learn everything he could about this Jesus he had committed to follow. Along the way he learned the importance of seeing the changes that need to be made in church, but recognizing that before they could change, he needed to work on that change in his own life first.

Through an extended process of research in New Testament Greek, Alan Knox came to understand that the way church is done today does not match what Scripture teaches. But rather than leave the church to "do it the right way," Alan decided to stay and help others within the church learn to live according to the true purpose, mission, and calling of the church.

Most church problems arise from power struggles within the leadership and ministry staff of a church. Sonny Lemmons witnessed this firsthand, and almost left his church as a result. But he decided to stay and help lead the church toward the love and unity that Jesus desired for his bride.

Travis Mamone recognized that the church is full of contradictions and problems. And while he toyed with the idea of leaving the church to follow Jesus, he decided to stay and rebuild the church from the inside out. He believes the way to do this is by focusing more and more on the church's one foundation, Jesus Christ our Lord.

Mary C. M. Phillips learned some insightful truths about life and church from an old Dodge Challenger that her mother drove. Through it, she saw the hypocrisy of Christians, but also saw that only Jesus is perfectly reliable, and that sometimes, loving others is more important than going to church.

Bill Reichart was brought on staff at a church as the Pastor of Assimilation. He was tasked with helping people connect to others in the church, and find fulfillment and meaning in serving there. Initially, they tried to start small groups as a way to encourage connections, but when this failed, Bill had to step back and take a fresh look at what it means to be Christ's church. He discovered that true unity and fulfillment in church comes from embarking on a mission together to love and serve others in the community.

In her darkest moment and deepest need, Aubry Smith was abandoned and rejected by the church. For a while, she returned the favor and stayed away. But she eventually returned to help lead the church into maturity as faithful and loving followers of Jesus Christ.

John Walker was part of a church that undertook a massive building project, and then watched most of the people in their church lose their jobs and move away. Faced with crushing debt and limited prospects, the church decided to focus on the one thing they could: loving and serving other people. As they did this, God provided for the church in amazing ways, and they are now debt free and are a beacon of light to all the people in their community.

After Markus Watson became the pastor of a struggling and dying church, he helped the church navigate through the difficult transition of combining a contemporary service with a traditional one. He tells what he did and how the people of the church responded, and how this experience taught him to rely on God for all future changes that are needed in the church.

CHAPTER 24
BEING THE CHANGE I WANT TO SEE

By Alan E. Brisco

Looking for a perfect church? I'm not. There's no point.

As the old aphorism goes, "It wouldn't be perfect the moment I walked in." And it's a pretty good bet that whomever I'd find there would have satisfied the imperfection criteria already, without any help from me. That's one of the paradoxical things about the Church: we must admit the imperfection of this remarkable organism — *and* — not be okay with leaving it the way it is. So, some folks consciously stay within the Church while identifying, advocating, and advancing "alternative realities." I am one of these people. Well, sort of.

Change isn't easy, whether prompted from within or prodded from without. As many have pointed out, the church has difficulty dealing with change. This is ironic too, isn't it? After all, much of what we do, or at least are supposed to be doing, is to call people to change. You'd think we could get it right ourselves. Not so, it seems.

For years, I helped people in corporations process change. Of course, corporations have bosses with compensatory power to buy compliance. And, the stakes aren't as high when we're only talking about careers and money. More recently, I help the Church — and churches — engage change better, seeking to avoid all-to-common fractures and fissures while helping spiritual communities experience newness. Yet my close familiarity with church change doesn't make me (or my wife or children) immune to the angst and heartache of disruptive experiences, devastated emotions, or the disheartening dislocation of communal exile. We have known all of these realities in the most personal ways. Reform, change, even newness takes its tolls, whatever we call it. I write as someone who knows firsthand what its like to be one of those who's left a church and one who's seen others go. We've been the newbies; and we've welcomed newer newbies into community. We've been hurt; and we've been healed.

As I write these words my wife and I are "in between." We're in the time when we've left what we knew but haven't arrived at the place we will know and be known. Just over a year ago we left good people for good reasons that I won't list here. I did cite our reasons in an email to the senior minister. He replied that he understood, yet claimed, "now isn't the time to discuss these things." I wondered when might be a good time. I still haven't heard. I don't think I ever will.

If needed reforms are going to occur in the Church some people are going to have to be willing to talk with each other; respectfully and candidly... not all gussied up and pretending all is well. We're going to have to talk about finding newness, about finding the Church. We're going to have to address, on an ongoing basis, needed reforms—because God's all about newness.

In the past year we've visited a variety of churches; but we've not settled yet. Why? Well, things seem askew in ways that aren't always easy to describe. It's not that there aren't many good things in these churches. It's just that important things are missing, mutated, or seemingly muffled. They need reforms. You don't need to belong to see the signs.

We don't think we're better, smarter, or more spiritual than anyone else. We know enough to know that's not true. We believe God will plant us in a place where people are keen to experience newness and to contribute to reforming the Church, by participating within a community of fervent Jesus-followers. We're just not convinced that the next community will look or feel like ones we've been in before. The world is changing; so is the Church. We are changing too.

WHAT DOES IT TAKE TO BE A REFORMER?

Being a reformer isn't easy. Take a look at history. Reformers are met with blank stares, pursed lips, marginalization, and character assassination. All these and worse are common experiences for reformers when people's stations or statuses seem threatened. Good people can do bad things. So why rankle the ranks? Why not leave well enough alone? Who needs the hassles?

This is where I've experienced deep soul searching. I don't like to ruffle feathers or stir waters any more than the next person. I don't want to upset people. I don't want to be doubted or disliked. I am not a glutton for punishment. It's tempting in the midst of some situations to confuse preserving a pretense of peace with living peaceably. What do you do when the need for reform makes cruise control untenable?

In *Finding our Way Again*, Brian McLaren described it this way:

> "One of our most common temptations is to turn the way into a place, to turn the adventure into a status, to trade the runway for the hangar, to turn the path into a sitting room — even when we call it a sanctuary. When the movement becomes an institution, those whose hearts call them to pilgrimage get restless."[2]

Janice and I found ourselves in an institution and yes, we were restless. The question wasn't whether to move, but how to move. We knew that whatever we did, we might not come out looking good. Some people would not understand. Some people would choose not to understand. Some would understand and claim not to know. Some would know and practice selective memory. Such is a reality when you are identified with reform.

What's always at risk for a reformer, maybe even more than others, is the danger of losing the vibrancy and vitality of intimate relationship with Jesus. When you're contemplating and working through reform. It seems you're always in someone's crosshairs. All this can distract you. You can easily

---

[2] McLaren, Brian. *Finding Our Way Again: The Return to the Ancient Practices.* Nashville: Thomas Nelson, 2008.

get your mind and your heart on something other than the main thing. Yet no reform is ever so necessary as to require a person to compromise his or her character or break precious bonds of intimacy with Christ.

We knew from experience that posturing, pretense, and politics wastes time, drains energies, and kills hope. Participation in reform can corrupt you if you're not careful. A person's vertical relationship can take a battering while their horizontal relationships die from neglect. We've seen it. We've experienced it. We know you have to watch carefully to avoid becoming the very thing you are hoping to see changed.

When a person is called to be a reformer, the person needs to keenly remember Ephesians 4:1-3. Regardless of how urgent or compelling a reform may seem, the call to conduct ourselves worthily, demonstrating humility, gentleness, patience, and tolerance for one another in love, and diligence to preserve the unity of the Spirit will *never be outweighed* by any need for reform. I try to keep in mind that God will never call me to be less of him to accomplish more of anything. So, sometimes when others want a tug of war, the worthy response may be to not pick up the rope. Then, without a 'rope in hand', God may direct me to stay and stand still. He may call me to go elsewhere, as he did a year ago. Whatever God calls me to do; what is most important is conduct, not conquest. I don't need anyone to validate me, except God. Whether arriving, leaving or in between, anyone who's looking objectively must be able to see Christ in me. Otherwise I've failed. Ephesians 4:1-3 is the litmus test for reformers.

WHAT NEEDS TO BE REFORMED?

I don't pretend to know all the answers. I don't even know all the questions. Yet I do detect a shift in what Jesus-followers value and what the next generation of his disciples seeks. Much of what is done in many churches today won't fly. Why? It just doesn't pass muster. As Janice and I look for a place to call our church home, we've got some idea of what we're looking for, even if it's in an embryonic stage. We're also hoping to help nurture these reforms. Below are five of the reforms we hope for most.

First, we long for true Christian community. Christian community isn't hanging out around the sandwich table talking about things everyone's already agreed upon. That's not Christian community; that's a country club. Real, God-honoring, God-proving community involves more than assembling with people just like us.

God-witnessing community brings diverse people together, not around themselves, but around Jesus, not around their preferences, but around missional possibilities of Christ's mission. That's the real witness to the world; people choosing to be together who don't belong together; and living life well. When there's no explanation for people to be together, and when what's binding them together is the sweet, gentle breath of the Holy Spirit, then people outside watch and wonder and whisper, "See how they love each other." This is the kind of community for which we long. The Triune God exists in community. Each of us is formed in God's image, *Imago Dei*. We're created to thrive in that kind of community, bursting with life.

Second, we desire less focus on programs and performance. Whatever event a church can produce, the world can match it and likely outdo it. This was even true in the days of Jesus. At one point in his ministry, Jesus fed 20,000 or so people. About the same time on that sunny afternoon, many miles to the northeast, a maniacal mass of 50,000 or more gathered in a theater to cheer on animal hunts, macabre spectacles, and gladiators fighting fiercely to the death.

If God on a hillside couldn't outdraw the savage spectacle, what makes us believe we can? Why do we persist in believing bigger crowds confirm God's presence? I'm not saying a big crowd is inherently wrong; I am saying a big crowd is not evidence of God's favor.

This leads to the third thing we want to see. We need to change the way we count. Recently in conversation with Reggie McNeal, he remarked, "We ask 'Who's here?' God asks 'Who's missing?'" I want to be part of a church that uses different math. Let's recalibrate the way we measure "success."

Fourth, we long to belong to a community where people pray. About a year ago we had friends over for dinner. At the end of the night, as our friends were getting ready to leave, the man suggested we pray together. We sat down and took turns praying, each expressing gratitude to God, recalling God's character and his works, asking God to meet others' needs, praying for our broken society, and yes, asking God to meet our own needs, some of which hadn't been known to each other until voiced there in prayer. The prayer time didn't seem as long as it was. We were talking with God together and it was good. We called the time "social prayer." Our spirits long to be part of church with an uncommon reputation, "people of prayer."

Fifth, we want to see mission integrated into the life of the church. The late Robert Webber once told me, "Alan, if you've got hungry people living within five miles of your church, you're not really worshipping until you've made sure those people are fed." There are many types of hunger. Some hunger for food, others hunger for justice, while still others hunger for peace or love. Too often, churches feel they must choose between social issues and spiritual needs. But people need both. We long for a church that is passionate about loving people by doing things as Jesus did: meeting social needs and sharing the Good News with others.

WHAT NOW?

In the end, we want to be where the community's currency is love, faith, and hope, not cash, contacts, and credentials. Whatever the worship style, we want to worship in services where people experience awe, delight, truth, and hope. We want a place where people talk about the majesty of God, the beauty of Jesus, and aren't afraid or ashamed to refer to the Holy Spirit.

You may think we're asking too much. Is it possible to find a church like this?

We think we will. There are millions of others who are looking for something similar, and eventually God is bound to bring some of us together so we can be his church in the world as he desires.

CHAPTER 25
LOVE LOST AND FOUND

By Kris Camealy

Sitting in the pew, I leaned back against the hard wood, grumbling inside about the annoying discomfort of such a plain bench. Of all the things to grouse about, my heart settled on my physical discomfort that morning. The pew was not the issue. My irritation with my church had been growing for months. I also knew that while I thundered at my husband on the way home for meatier sermons, the Pastor wasn't the real issue either. For months I'd balked at our church. I could find twenty-five things on a good Sunday morning to moan about, and in my discontent, I longed to leave. Each week I'd compare what I'd heard from other nearby churches with what was happening within my own church. I came starving every Sunday morning only to leave unfilled, and more irritated.

A HUNGER FOR MORE

I had numerous complaints about our church. It's too traditional. It's so stuffy. The congregation feels dead. No one is willing to help out. The longer my complaints list grew, the more I hungered to go somewhere else, somewhere more "on fire," somewhere where the pastor ripped in to the lazy congregation and challenged them to get up and live the message of Christ, for Pete's sake. Annoyance and irritation transitioned into anger over the lack of energy and enthusiasm within my own church. Where was everyone's passion? I grew both sad and resentful. Sitting Sunday after Sunday on that hard bench I'd dream about leaving but having been at the church a handful of years, my children had made friends—their roots sinking deeper and deeper each week. Could I really just demand we switch churches—just because our congregation lacked a passion for Christ that I hungered for? I couldn't do it.

My fingers curled tightly around that yellow printed bulletin, the announcements that morning filled with dire needs—ministries using words like "desperate for volunteers" and "extremely urgent." There was so much unmet need. The list of those who serve may as well be carved in stone because for years it's the same handful of people, giving until they've lost their zeal and grown tired from always being the one to show up.

I wanted to leave because I wanted to be fed. I wanted to switch churches because in my selfishness, I neglected to consider what my role ought to be—that perhaps I should be one who helps feed, rather than waiting to be fed. My own bitterness and resentment swelled as I stared at the pleas for help. Scanning the sanctuary I counted the various heads of people who I never saw other than Sunday morning. Where were they? Why, in a church with over 250 members, were we "desperate" for volunteers?

I'd been Reading David Platt's *Radical* and Francis Chan's *Crazy Love* and both books left me hungry to experience a more fierce faith in the pews around me. I wanted more of this wild Gospel; I wanted to attend a church that burned brighter, a church with more active members that shared my hunger for Christ's hard challenges. I wanted my pastor to run the gauntlet and challenge my fellow congregants. I wanted to rub elbows on Sunday with real people, not the masked ones in their sport coats and pearls.

I fantasized about worshipping in a church unafraid to preach the radical message of grace to a bunch of equaling starving believers who boldly let their "Amens" and "Hallelujahs" fly from the pew. I wanted to lift my hands during worship and not feel like a pariah. I wanted to see tissue boxes at the ends of pews because by the time the message hit your hearts, mid-sermon, you were going to need them. Sunday morning in my conservative Lutheran church held none of this for me, and looking around the sanctuary, my resentment swelled. I grew increasingly bitter—until God cracked my ugly heart wide open.

THE WORK OF GOD

About the time my frustration peeked, God went to work on me in a way I didn't see coming. Ripping back the layers of my resentment He exposed me to my own shortcomings. Over the next year He shaped and molded me from a complaining pew warmer, into an active ministry leader—a role I neither deserved nor was truly prepared for. In all my fuming about wanting to leave this church, God's conviction came swift and certain.

While I'd been racking up a list of grievances against my fellow body God quickly called me to the carpet for my own offenses. I had lost my love for this church. The words of 1 Corinthians 13:2 convicted me repeatedly during this difficult season: "If I… have not love, I am nothing." God didn't want me to leave this church; he wanted me to serve it.

When the opportunity to coordinate MOPS for my church fell into my lap, I knew this was God's way of giving me a second chance. Here I now had the opportunity to serve, to get past my frustration by learning what it means to have a servant's heart. I accepted the opportunity with no hesitation, but several misgivings. With a year behind me, I'm still finding my footing. I live and breathe by 2 Corinthians 12:9, which says, "My power is made perfect in weakness." I'm counting on it because I am weak.

I could have left the church. I could have taken up with a more obviously radical bunch of active Christians and worshipped with my hands in the air and tears on my cheeks. But God had another idea in mind. He spun me right around on my ear and called me to serve the very congregation I no longer loved.

BEGINNING TO LOVE AGAIN

Christ's truth reveals to me again and again that if I want to be served, I need to serve first. The gospel message isn't about worship styles—it's about getting low and washing feet. I began to pray for my Pastor, something I should have been doing, but ashamedly, wasn't. I learned more stories behind the scenes about my fellow members of the body, and I began to see glimpses of the faith I'd been longing for. Quietly, without fully realizing it, I began to love again.

I'd lost my way and the only way back would be a slow crawling on my knees. Looking back at the experience it saddens me how I allowed the bitterness to root and grow unchecked. My prideful arrogance led me to misunderstand and disrespect my church and the body it's made of. Things aren't perfect, we still struggle immensely with volunteers and I'm still neck deep in figuring out how to run a ministry with humility and grace but God broke my heart for my congregation in a way I didn't anticipate. He is the very definition of love and in learning to love again, I find myself reflecting a fraction more of him and a little less of me. I didn't need a new church. I needed a new heart for my own church home.

Wiping tears from my eyes last Sunday I knew I was right where I belonged. Whispering "amen" as the sermon ends, I press back against the hard pew, uncurling the bulletin in my hands, I scan for another opportunity to serve, drawing a thin blue line under the request, I tuck the yellow paper into my purse and shake my pastors hand on the way out the door, "See you next week," I affirm to him.

CHAPTER 26
THE CHURCH IS MESSY, BUT YOU CAN'T LIVE WITHOUT HER

By Daniel Darling

It was a church continually beset by controversy. The pastor's delivery was fairly dour. His sermons railed against the new social customs embraced by the young people in his community. The mission of the church was too closely synched with politics, as Christian leaders pushed their favorite officials for appointment to high office and government officials routinely intervened in the affairs of the churches. New music styles split old guard from new. And para-church movements threatened the local control of established evangelical parishes.

It was a chaotic scene, filled with disillusioned followers of Christ, quarreling church leaders, and theological fistfights. In some ways, it could be almost any 21st century evangelical church.

But it isn't. It's the climate of the famous church in Northampton, Massachusetts pastored by America's best-known theologian, Jonathan Edwards. The troubled situation in Northampton eventually led to the dismissal of this legendary American patriarch, and his situation echoes some of the ugliness we see in today's evangelical church.

But it also gives me hope that the problems we see in churches across the land are troublesome, but not intractable; deep, but not permanent; vexing, but not all-powerful. And if you study church history from the pages of the book of Acts until the current, if you can avoid the sort of hazy, rose-colored, revisionist perspectives, you'll find that the church has always had problems. This is mainly because the church is always full of humans, inflicted since birth with the desire and propensity to sin, especially against one another.

CHURCH RELEVANCE

Today there is a lot of talk about the relevance of the church. Do we still need it? Does it even answer the vexing problems that face our world? Are we so isolated that the cultural issues are being shaped without our voice? Can I still find God in church? In our media-saturated world, can I faithfully follow Jesus *ala Carte*, choosing my spiritual diet from a variety of diverse offerings?

Perhaps I'm in the minority in my generation. Perhaps I speak to folks who've already decided that the hierarchy and bureaucracy of Protestant religion is too clumsy to change. But still I want to make the argument that our spiritual life with God thru Christ is not only helped by participation in a local expression of Christ's church, but will suffocate and die without it.

THE BRIDE HE LOVES

The Scripture use a variety of metaphors to describe the church, but perhaps the most compelling is the one of a bride. In Ephesians 5:25-27, the Apostle Paul says that the church was purchased with a great sacrifice by Christ. In fact, Paul uses the human union of a man and woman as an illustration of Christ's union with his bride. Even the beauty of human marital intimacy and oneness pales in comparison to the love Christ expresses for his church.

Christ, as the faithful husband, not only sacrificed his body and loves his bride, but he has not given up on her. He will not abandon her. Matthew 16:18 quotes Jesus as saying that the "gates of hell" (KJV) shall not prevail over the church. Yes, the clumsy institution, whose death has been predicted in every generation, will not die. Not because of her clever programs or cultural relevance, but because Christ has determined that his bride will prevail.

In fact, it is for the bride that Christ returns at the end of the age, defeats the nations, and establishes his kingdom. He is coming back for his bride (Rev 19:7-9; 21:1-2).

Jesus loves the church. Jesus died for the church. Jesus ensures the survival of the church. Jesus will return one day for his church. So, if Jesus loves the church, we too must love the church. Not simply the people in the church with whom we agree or the church we wish we would see, but the church as it currently is express. Jesus loves us, warts and all, mistakes, failures, and blind spots.

So before you think about abandoning the church, remember that Jesus hasn't abandoned it. He loves her and calls you to love her too.

THE PLACE WHERE JESUS DWELLS

The church is not only Jesus' bride, but she is also the place where Jesus most often dwells (Matt 18:2). That's not to say it's the only place Jesus dwells. He also dwells in every believer by faith through the Holy Spirit (Eph 1:14). However, you can't read much of the New Testament without seeing that God's purposes in this age are to work through the church, his body. The church is the expression of Jesus in the world (John 17; Matt 16:18).

In his final words to his disciples, Jesus made the outrageous statement that they would do "greater things" than he (John 14:12). In other words, the presence of the Holy Spirit in the hearts of his followers would have a wider impact than Jesus present, earthly ministry.

But you may look upon the worldwide church with dismay. You may say, as some, that we've drifted so far from our mission. And yet our effectiveness is not dependent necessarily on our faithfulness, but on the faithfulness of Jesus to work through us to accomplish his will in the world before he comes as reigning King.

This is why your spiritual life must be engaged in the church, because you cannot live for Jesus apart from his mission and you cannot accomplish your mission apart from the church. Life in Christ is never simply a vertical relationship with you and God; it is always both vertical and horizontal. Your faith is measured both by personal piety and soul-to-soul relationships with other people. You cannot love Christ without loving your brother (Mark 12:31; 1 John 3).

Furthermore, the Scriptures teach us that our gifts are specifically given to us, not for our own spiritual edification, but so we can use them to serve God's church (Eph 4). In other words, simply engaging the spiritual disciplines without applying them in service toward other believers in the church cuts off the believer from His mission and full experience as a called-out member of Christ's church.

SINNERS ON MISSION

Perhaps it's time we viewed the church differently. We often look at church in terms of our unmet expectations, the flaws, blind spots, and grievances. And while those may be real, it's important to understand that each church you join, no matter how dynamic the leadership, how effective the ministries, how powerful the preaching—will be comprised of sinners. If you develop deep relationships, at some point in your experience, another Christian will hurt you. And you will hurt one or more as well. This is part of the messy, human experience. And yet in the Church, perhaps more than any other institution, you have the opportunity to grow more like Jesus by experiencing the full range of temptation, testing, and trial. You'll experience grace and forgiveness and repentance.

It is true that if you never engage fully in the body life of church, you will minimize your opportunity for spiritual abuse, you'll shield yourself from relational hurt by other believers, and you'll be safe from the bad stuff churches can foist on each other. But you'll also miss the unique opportunity to allow God's Spirit to breathe life through you into the lives of those others similarly journeying toward heaven. You'll miss the joy of utilizing your unique giftedness to give back to Christ's beloved body. And your impact on the world for the glory of Jesus' name will be severely limited.

Ultimately we grow disappointed with the church because it fails to meet every need, it falls short of our expectations. But perhaps what we want from a church may not be what Jesus intended her to give us. Perhaps we expect a level of satisfaction and perfection that only Christ can provide. It may be time to readjust our expectations and instead view our local body of believers as fellow sinners on mission, souls for whom Jesus died, and the blood-bought saints he has called me to serve.

If you want your life to be lasting, your impact to be eternal, serve the only institution guaranteed by Christ to last forever. Engage his church.

CHAPTER 27
A STORY OF BECOMING

By Melody Harrison Hanson

When I began attending my church ten years ago, I had a cavernous hole in my heart. I was a casualty of a cruel and angry father, and as a result, my understanding of God was distorted and my faith in shambles. I longed for love and connection. I wanted to believe that I was loved. But though I hoped, I did not believe. Despite my uncertainties, it was in this new community that Jesus met me, and began putting me back together. It was here, in this place *of doing and being* the church that I found restoration and experienced a holy transformation. This church has been a place of *becoming something new*.

Within this community I have learned of Christ's grace and because of that I can receive and give love. I finally found the freedom and peace of being loved by God.

To be honest, I resisted this particular local church. As a feminist, with an egalitarian hermeneutic and radar for bigotry, I was uncomfortable with their lack of female pastors, teachers, and elders. On the surface, the church appeared to hold hierarchal views. I was drawn to the vibrant and authentic intellectual community, with worship that was sacred and stimulating, yet I knew I would have to compromise theologically.

In the contemporary church we are so used to hearing and seeing men, we keep women silent Sunday after Sunday. Women are spectators, recipients, and the beneficiaries. To stay in my church, I had to figure out if there was a greater purpose than my individual story. What was my place in the biblical story, even as I am certain that women should use every gift and talent they have been given by a generous God?

My teenage daughter, who sees what is in our church imagines that this is the way it is supposed to be. If our church were wrong, why would we stay? And friends in other church traditions often challenge me that change may never happen until women (and men) are willing to take their money and their feet elsewhere. But my church is so big that I don't believe leaving would make a whit of difference. Perhaps there is a greater purpose to staying, but staying and waiting for change can be so difficult.

DREAM DEFERRED

Langston Hughes once asked, "What happens to a dream deferred?" I wonder what damage is done when our ideals are deferred, when the truth we most long to see realized is recurrently overdue? My heart aches for genuine equality for women in the church. I have long dreamt of beautiful things we will do when that happens.

But what was I doing in this place of dreams deferred? Part of the answer to that question lies in my own tension on the subject of women in the church. Simply put, I have not been certain, living as we are in the midst of the great debate occurring today, with churches being split along denominational and theological lines. Because of the divide, many of those with strong egalitarian views tend to gravitate to denominations that actively affirm women. While this is understandable, it prevents the discussion that might occur if those voices were not absent. The flight of egalitarians also has the effect that more moderate or conservative communities tend to sink deeper into the "Complementarian" view, with their masculine God and clearly demarcated roles for men and women.

When churches are divided on this slippery topic and the Bible seems to reveal the "dream deferred" how does the layperson know where to stand, let alone how *to stand firm?*

WOMEN IN SCRIPTURE

Scot McKnight, a respected New Testament scholar suggests in his book *Blue Parakeet,* rather than look in Scripture for what women cannot or should not do; we should instead ask, what *did* women do?[3] Following McKnight's lead, I marveled as I read the New Testament stories of women leading churches, preaching and prophesying, and taking up roles that *their culture* clearly never *conferred upon them*. There are accounts in Scripture to support the gender hierarchies of the time. To argue that the Bible is either fully egalitarian or fully patriarchal ignores the culture of the day, which was a messy and unclear context.

The voices of women in Scripture were subdued by culture and interpretation. Just take Junia, the New Testament Apostle, whom translators have maintained for generations, was a man. Scot McKnight's essay, *Junia is Not Alone,* confirmed my suspicion that this interpretation is subjective and biased. I also became more inclined to study Scripture for myself.[4]

In the New Testament, a woman boldly poured an anointing of perfume over Jesus in the home of Simon the Leper. Opening a bottle, bravely and for a higher purpose, she poured it on Jesus' head. She anointed him when no one else did, even as others were indignant over her brazen and highly irregular actions. Jesus, who could have rejected or ignored her, told them to leave her alone (Mark 14:3-9). He then praised her actions, and said that what she had done would be told everywhere.

Jesus expected that her story would be told and her act of courageous worship would be admired. This woman, in a time when women were not allowed, risked public ridicule and rejection, stepped out of all of the comforts and protection of her culture, and showed her love to Jesus. And Jesus affirmed her for doing so!

Jesus also appeared to two women after his resurrection, at a time when testimony from women was illegitimate. Why? He valued their witness.

---

3   McKnight, Scot. *The Blue Parakeet: Rethinking How You Read the Bible.* Grand Rapids: Zondervan, 2008.
4   McKnight, Scot. *Junia is Not Alone.* Englewood, CO: Patheos, 2011.

Jesus' story included a woman's brave worship and anointing. It included the witness of women to his resurrection. I wonder why? Jesus took risks for women, ministered with, received from and listened to women. Don't you wonder why? I believe it is because he is our example of reconciliation and grace. I believe the church needs the spiritual voices of women.

FINDING MY VOICE

I've considered asking God to take it away—this feminist awareness—to either shut it up or *get me out of this particular church; but* for now I stay, finding my voice, learning and listening, studying, so that I have something solid and circumspect to contribute.

Today in my church, women still don't preach, still can't be elders, and no one will say publicly what they believe about women. But my church is open-minded. They care about women. They work to have a woman on the platform in worship. They do not restrict women from serving on committees, and women definitely outnumber men in general contribution. Women do direct program areas. And though women cannot be ordained in the denomination, in my church they call these women pastors if they have seminary training.

Though the broader church is divided and denominations split over lesser things, I look to the arc of the Story of God and I believe that Jesus liberates us all, men and women, to use all of our gifts in the Kingdom of God. Although our denomination has not caught up, my church *practices* an affirmation of women serving out of (almost all of) their gifts, and more importantly, encourages us to *actively live out our faith, love Jesus, one another, and our community.* It is beautiful, it is radical, and this *community* sustains my faith as we pray for one another, serve together, confess our sin, and accept one another unconditionally. Because of this community, I am not the same person. Because of this, I stay, I love, I hope, and I dream.

CHAPTER 28
BEING THE CHANGE I WANT TO SEE

By Dan King

"Alright, so what now?"

That was pretty much my first thought moments after stepping forward one Sunday morning and accepting God's call. I was 28 years old, and I was ready to commit myself to this Christianity thing once and for all. I lived totally for me for just about every bit of that first 28 years. Now it was time for a change, and that change started at the altar on an otherwise ordinary Sunday morning.

CHRISTIAN CLICHÉS

While I was ready to make the change in my life, I had no idea what it was supposed to look like. People would drop all the usual Christian clichés on me, but most of that didn't change my life in any way.

"You can do all things through Christ who strengthens you!"

I wasn't sure how exactly Jesus would strengthen me, nor did I know what it was that I needed him to do. I was still pretty new to Christianity, and spent a lot of my life figuring out how to do the things I could do under my own strength.

"You're more than a conqueror!"

I'm a conqueror? Of what? All of life's worries and problems? Last time I checked, just believing that I was "more than a conqueror" didn't take any of my problems away.

"Now you'll get to spend eternity in heaven worshiping God!"

This is one of my favorites. I don't know about you, but I still have a hard time picturing this one. Lots of people like to refer to the luxuries that come with this cliché, like the streets of gold, or being in the awesome house that Jesus has built. The reality is that we know very little about what heaven will actually look like, so it was hard for me to get how this reality was supposed to change me here and now.

The more clichés I heard from other people, the more apparent it became to me that I'd have to work this thing out myself. So I set out to be a student of The Book and of the church culture that I found myself suddenly immersed in.

CALIBRATING MYSELF WITH THE WORD

To learn what I needed to know, I embarked upon a three-year Bible reading plan, which I called "the fives." It wasn't a typical beginning-to-end reading plan, or even a fancy chronological schedule. Rather, it was a systematic study that was designed to immerse me in the content every Christian should know. The entire plan would take me through the whole Bible eventually, but there were also times when I'd have to read the same Epistle (completely) every day for an entire month. So there were many parts of the Bible that I read several times as I worked through the plan at an average pace of five chapters per day.

To this day, I still believe that this experience as a "baby" Christian was one of the most formative experiences I could have gone through. And one thing is for sure; I quickly discovered where all of those Christian clichés came from!

I also realized how out of context most Christians were taking many of the statements they threw around.

SERMONETTE SLOGANS

The lack of Bible knowledge today is not anyone's fault in particular. It is more a reflection of the culture we've been buried in for years. The evening (and now 24-hour) news is a source of sharing quick, important highlights of the story. As a result, we've started processing the Bible and sermons in a similar fashion. If most of us are lucky, we walk away from a Sunday service with one or two key statements or slogans that define the entire message that our pastors are sharing with us.

This has had several obvious impacts on many of us in the church. Because people have been able to rely on getting their sound bites on Sunday mornings to carry them through their Christian lifestyles, the church as a whole has become Biblically illiterate.

So the big question is, "How can the church ever reach its potential if its members don't know (or even understand) the Word?" After all, a theology based on sound bites can never sustain real change and long-term transformation in a Christian's life.

THE BEST PERSON FOR THE JOB

I was sitting in a job interview with a man I was terrified to talk to. I respected him a great deal, but he intimidated me. And this one man's thoughts about our conversation determined whether or not I got the job. So I had to make it count.

To my surprise, much of the interview felt more like a conversation between old friends. We had worked on some projects in the past, and like a trip down memory lane, we recalled some of our experiences working together. We had a good laugh over some of the meeting and events that happened early on, and we congratulated each other over some of the successes we've shared. Then he asked me the question that stuck with me well beyond that interview: "If you were me, and there was something in hindsight that you would do differently on this project, what would it be?"

Fortunately for me, this was a question that I was ready to answer. And in that moment, I felt comfortable answering it with every bit of honesty that it deserved. We ended up having a great conversation about things that I would have done differently if I could go back, and things that I wish the rest of the team could have done better to support the project from the viewpoint that I had. I laid it all out, and he nodded in agreement as he listened intently as I shared my heart.

"Those are some great observations," he said to me. "You know, someone told me once that the best person for the job is usually the one who sees the most that needs to be changed. In a sense, it's like saying, 'Congratulations, now go fix it.'"

Guess who got the job?

In my new role, that perspective became the centerpiece of everything that I did. I had set out to bring the change that I saw that needed to happen. And it meant that if I wanted to see things change, then it would have to start with me.

BECOMING THE CHANGE I WANT TO SEE

The mindset of fixing me first infiltrated everything that I do. If I wanted a better marriage, then I first need to be a better husband. If I want to have better kids, then I should be thinking about how I can be a better dad. And if I want to see a better church, then I need to figure out how to be a better Christian.

Shane Claiborne and Jonathan Wilson-Hartgrove talked about this idea in their book, *Becoming the Answer to Our Prayers*. It's a book about how we are the answer to our prayers. If we pray that God would feed the hungry, then it's us who are the ones who have the ability to be the fulfillment of those prayers. In the book, they made a statement that couldn't make this idea any more clear...

> *When we pray to God asking, "Why don't you do something?" we hear a gentle whisper respond, "I did do something. I made you." Prayer is important. Just as important is the call to become the answer to our prayers.*[5]

---

5   Claiborne, Shane and Jonathan Wilson-Hartgrove. *Becoming the Answer to our Prayers: Prayer for Ordinary Radicals*. Downers Grove: IVP, 2008.

No other concept has driven me in my faith as much as this one. In a church culture full of clichés and sound bites, I've first had to strive to dig deeper in order to discover the voice of Truth and to hear the heartbeat of God.

I found the answer to my "What now?" question. And it's not an answer that lays anywhere else except between the Word of God and me. It's in the reality that if I chase after the Truth, and set myself apart to live that Truth the best that I can figure out how to, then I'll be the change that I want to see.

Before I can change anything or anyone else, I first have to change myself.

CHAPTER 29
PART OF THE CONTINUAL WORK OF REFORMING THE CHURCH

By Alan Knox

I grew up in the traditional churches of the southern part of the United States. I continued as part of these same churches throughout my young adult life. I knew the church as an organization, an event, or a special building used by these organizations for these events. Yes, people were part of that organization, but the organization was the church. Half the people could leave—as occasionally happened—but the organization, and thus the church, would continue.

I do not say this with animosity. I do not hate the times that I spent as part of these organizations. There were great people in these church organizations, and many of them helped me grow as a follower of Jesus Christ. I was never hurt by these organizations, but to the contrary, I thrived in those environments, even taking on various roles and functions and leadership responsibilities.

SEMINARY TRAINING FOR THE MINISTRY

About ten years ago, my family moved to another state so that I could attend seminary in order to continue serving in more important positions in those kinds of church organizations. I planned to get a job with one of these organizations as one of the staff pastors. Of course, at that time, I would not have put my goal in those terms. Instead, I would have said that I was called into the ministry, that I was training for the ministry, and that I would be seeking a call to a local church. I planned to graduate from seminary as soon as possible and find a job in a local church.

For the most part, I completely enjoyed my time at seminary. I am naturally a very studious and academic person. Writing comes easy for me. I am quite good at memorizing and remembering information. I do not say these things to brag; it simply describes how I am made, and it shows that I am the kind of person that our educational system—including seminaries—is designed for.

Something surprising happened during my time in seminary. I found that I loved studying languages, especially Greek. As part of my curriculum, I had to take two courses in *Koine* Greek (the Greek that was used to write the New Testament). After taking those two courses, I wanted to continue. So, for the remainder of my time in seminary, I took classes in Greek language, Greek documents, and Greek exegesis (translation and interpretation).

Through this study, I found that there were occasionally disconnects between what the text of Scripture said and how we tend to interpret it and live it out. When I would ask about this disconnect, I would sometimes get an answer such as, "That's not the way things are done today."

While I understood that there are social and cultural differences between us and the authors of the New Testament, I also began to understand some of the differences that I was noticing were not simply differences of culture, but were differences in purpose and identity. Of course, I was not the only one who noticed these differences, and many people (including some of my seminary professors) were asking people to considering how they used certain words, such as "church," or "minister," or "pastor."

NEW UNDERSTANDING TO OLD TERMS

"Church" was a big one for me. I knew that the English term "church" was used to translate the Greek term *ekklesia*. But, I began to realize more and more that people today did not use the term "church" in the same way that the authors of the New Testament used the term *ekklesia*. Our misuse of the term "church" was causing us to misunderstand what Scripture was saying about the church—the *ekklesia*.

I began to recognize that those organizations and institutions that I always associated with the term "church" were not actually the church at all. The church is people—the people of God who have been saved by faith in Jesus Christ and have been indwelled by the Holy Spirit of God. The people who are part of the same "local church" organization are part of the church, even though the organization is not the church. But, in the same way, the people who lived in the same neighborhood as me— the people that I waved at and spoke to occasionally—were also part of the church if they are also in Christ. My coworkers—the people who I spent the most time with week in and week out— were also part of the church if they are also in Christ.

It is Jesus Christ and the indwelling of his Spirit that makes us members of the body of Christ, members of one another, and part of the church together. The fact that we do not live as the church together or recognize each other as the church does not change our identity as the church. These are my brothers and sisters in Christ. I do not get to pick and choose who will be part of the church with me. God has already chosen and has already placed people in my life according to his plan and his will.

I slowly began to realize the massive implications of this. I began to understand that scriptural concepts such as unity, fellowship, service, and love would have to be completely reevaluated as well.

STAYING BUT REFORMING

It would have been easy to walk away from those organizations and institutions that identify themselves as "church." I had been part of those organizations for the long time, and it was easy to see the problems fostered by identifying the institutions as the church. But, there was one big problem. While I do not recognize those organizations as the church, I do recognize that the people involved in those organizations *are* the church. They are also people whom God has placed in my life, and he has placed me in their lives. Therefore, we need one another. I need them just as much as they need me.

So, in one sense, I do not see myself as "reforming the church." It is not my goal or purpose to walk into situations and organizations and point out what I think they are doing wrong or to show what they misunderstand about Scripture—not even to demonstrate their misunderstanding of the word "church."

Instead, it is my goal to live as a follower of Jesus Christ. This includes living as a brother with other followers of Jesus Christ—both with those who agree with me about the church and also with those who do not agree with me about the church. Sure, it is always easier to live with people who agree with you. But, as Paul exhorted, I am learning to consider others more important than myself, and I am finding that I can learn and grow from the example of those who remain part of those organizations and institutions. Why? Because they are also indwelled by the Holy Spirit.

So, in that sense, I do see myself continuing the work of "reforming the church." And, that continual reformation includes me. Because, I am also part of the church that continually needs to be reformed—changed by the power of God through the working of his Spirit through each follower of Jesus Christ.

Today, when I gather with a group of people regularly on Sunday mornings, we are the church, and, as we encourage one another toward maturity in Christ, we are reforming one another. When I run with a brother in the Lord and we help one another abide in Christ as we are running, we are the church, and we are reforming one another. When my family has dinner with some friends who are Christians and as our conversations exhort one another toward love and good works, we are the church, and together we are reforming the church. When I meet someone for coffee and we help one another walk in the Spirit, we are the church, and we are part of the continual work that God is doing to reform his church.

CHAPTER 30
THE RED TRUCK CONTINGENCY PLAN

By Sonny Lemmons

We jokingly called it "The Red Truck Contingency Plan."

The church I was serving in at the time (as an unpaid volunteer) had six ministers and one full-time administrative assistant. As such, each person on staff was integral to the day-to-day operations of their respective ministries, as well as ensuring that the worship services went smoothly for the several hundred individuals who called this their home.

The idea behind the Red Truck Contingency Plan arose one day when, as we were trying to plot out the next teaching series, we realized it was going to take place during the Senior Pastor's vacation. Typically, when we planned out our teaching series, we would come up with a thematic idea we wanted to focus on, and leave the details and heart of the talk to the Senior Pastor. At some point, someone on the Creative Team said that maybe we should go a little bit deeper into designing this series, since we would collectively be responsible for the content and delivery of the messages ourselves.

"After all," someone remarked, "who knows? One day, the Senior Pastor could be driving to church and "BOOM!" A big red pickup truck just sideswipes his car, killing him instantly. Sure, we could go on and have the church services that day, but wouldn't it be better if we all knew the specifics about what we needed to do after that?"

And so began the practice of communicating frequently and openly with each other more about their job functions and ministry tasks. The Family Pastor showed the Small Groups Pastor how things ran in his ministry. The Senior Pastor taught the Children's Pastor how things ran in his office. And in a trickle-down effect, those of us who were serving without monetary compensation found ourselves with some of the keys to this kingdom, learning the ins and outs of the ministry. This way, had anyone been "Red Trucked," their ministry could continue without skipping a beat.

The openness and loving spirit as we taught and learned was somewhat reminiscent of the story in Acts about beleivers gathering together to share their possessions. And just as we desire the beauty and comparative simplicity of the early church, so our church seemed beautiful, simple, and loving. For a while, it was a true expression and extension of the collaborative nature church could and should be.

THE CRASH

The problem with sharing with others how you do your ministry is that they soon have ideas for how you can do it better. Words like "fresh," "different," "exciting," and "enjoyable" are usually positive words. But they are viewed as critical condemnation when uttered by a well-meaning fellow staff person who has a "few suggestions" for improving your area of ministry.

Meetings to discuss upcoming sermons or lessons became less conversational and more task-centered and administratively based. Doors went back to being literally and figuratively closed. Those of us on the outside (of the payroll) were quickly relegated back to the role of observer. We were not of the inner circle, and therefore, found wanting.

We were, in a very real sense, "Red Trucked" by a large red truck named "Ego."

My question and struggle then became what to do. Could I go back to functioning in an environment that felt increasingly self-centered and potentially toxic? It was like some bizarre twist on a Thanksgiving experience: Could I go back and sit at the "Kid's Table" now that I knew what it was like to sit at the "Big Table?" Although I was invested in the lives of the people I served, I understood that if I left, my departure would hurt me more than anyone else. Nature abhors a vaccum, and if I left, someone else would quickly fill the empty ministry. The church would continue to function as usual, but I would be left alone, trying to find a new church where I could plug in and get involved. At least here, I had a role and a ministry.

So I stayed. And in staying, God taught me something important about the ministry and mission of the church.

RED TRUCKING THE MESSIAH

In our efforts to hold on to our vision for ministry, we "Red Trucked" the Messiah and used his message to manage to our own empires.

More often than not, the majority of the people who attend church services are not privy to the inner workings of their church. They may know their pastor or minister socially, but it is sometimes a completely different dynamic to serve with them in a co-leadership position than to be in a small group with them. Transparency and accountability are seemingly easier for some pastors to provide in terms of their personal life, but when it comes to the church, especially if it is their church, walls come up. Church leaders may play well together on Sundays, but act like a dysfunctional family the other six days of the week.

The majority of the scars and wounds I bear come not from the people who attend church but from the ones who run it. It's interesting that my pains don't come from words of hate or judgement spoken against me. Instead, my hurt comes from dealing with pastors who can't understand why they keep having such a massive turnover in staff or volunteers.

When Jesus told Peter to feed his sheep and tend his flock, the emphasis wasn't on who owned the sheep but on the action to be performed. Jesus commands us to feed and tend, but he didn't provide a three-step action plan with blanks for us to fill in according to a DVD series he authored. As the Bridegroom, he is protective of his bride, but he trusts us to set up the wedding feast as we see fit. Jesus managed to align himself with a crew of volunteers whom he entrusted to run things, acting in his name and on his authority when he left.

In our own ministries, the pasture I lead sheep to may have a different variety of grass growing on it than what someone else might feed them, but ultimately, it's grass all the same. We can be, and mostly are, drawn to the charisma and stylings of a particular teacher or pastor, because they speak to something similar inside us.

A LITTER BETTER

Robert Baden-Powell, the individual who began the Scouting movement, is credited with coming up with the slogan, "Leave the world a little better than you found it." This phrase managed to settle into my heart during this season as I struggled with what I was to do. Ultimately, I decided that staying was the right thing to do. I did not desire to stay out of a false sense of ego, thinking I had the right ideas and ways to implement them. Instead, I thought it was my responsibility to help build a healthy church for those who came after me. I wanted to leave this church a little better than I found it, and to accomplish this, I needed to stay. I had been brought to this church for a reason, and my season was not yet complete.

The church, both this specific body of believers, and the worldwide congregation, should be bigger than one person, one ministry, one mindset of order or style of worship. She should manifest and reflect inclusivity, love, and a willingness to adapt, grow and change.

That way, we can have "Red Truck" insurance that never expires.

CHAPTER 31
THE BRIDE WITH HOLES IN HER DRESS
By Travis Mamone

Someone once said, "The church is a whore, but that whore is the bride of Christ and your mother, and you have no right to abandon her." Indeed, the church and I have had a difficult relationship for years. I tried running away from her, but somehow or other I would always find myself falling on my knees before her, begging her to take me back. Frankly, I'm getting sick of this pattern. Something needs to change.

ENCOUNTERING GOD

I wasn't raised in the church. My parents weren't atheists or anything, but we never went to church unless someone died or someone got married. Yet whenever I stepped into a church, I always felt like I had just walked into a sacred place. The pews, the altar, the baptismal, and the hymnals—they all held mysterious powers that I wanted to explore.

Then in high school I did the whole prodigal son thing. I was the kid who dressed all in black, listened to Marilyn Manson, dabbled in Wicca, and sliced his arms with a razor blade. I was close to ending up in a mental ward when one night, while crying on the phone with my high school girlfriend Arlena, God finally caught up to me.

And thus began my dysfunctional relationship with the church.

DYSFUNTIONAL CHURCH

The first church I went to was the church that Arlena went to. For those familiar with the movie *The Apostle* with Robert Duvall, it was just like that. When the pastor prayed, the congregation responded with orgasmic "Ooh" and "Yes, Lord!" and spontaneously broke out into tongues. After about three years of feeling stuck in a Benny Hinn revival, I left that church and joined a megachurch.

The megachurch was a lot more laid-back than the tongue-talking church. The sanctuary looked more like a movie theater, the pastor wore Hawaiian shirts instead of a suit, the drama department performed skits before the sermon, and you could slip off your shoes in your seat if you wanted to. The sermons were usually topics like "How to manage time/money," and were full of quotable bullet points and bite-sized chunks of Scripture. Even though I was more comfortable in the megachurch than in the tongue-talking church, I still felt like something was missing, but I couldn't put my finger on it.

Then one day I started going to a Lutheran church and it suddenly hit me: I've been an in-the-closet Lutheran all this time! Unlike the tongue-talking church and the megachurch, the Lutheran church wasn't interested in putting on a show to keep congregants entertained. Instead, the liturgy was built around encountering Jesus' love through hymns, preaching, and communion. This particular church was part of the Missouri Synod, which is the more conservative branch of the American Lutheran church. They don't ordain women, they believe homosexuality is a sin, and they tend to interpret the Bible literally. At first that stuff didn't really bother me, but as my beliefs developed throughout the years I suddenly found myself at odds with many of the Missouri Synod's teachings. Things got even more complicated when I finally came out as bisexual.

For the past couple of months I've been attending an Evangelical Lutheran church. It has the beauty of the liturgy with the progressive attitude I've been searching for all this time. Yet even now that I've found a church I'm comfortable with, I still have a love/hate relationship with the church.

LOVE/HATE RELATIONSHIP

I love Jesus, but I don't know about his followers sometimes. If Jesus said, "He who lives by the sword dies by the sword," why did so many evangelical Christians support the war in Iraq? Why do so many Christians think homosexuality is the worst thing in the world, yet hardly blink an eye at corporate greed? Why doesn't "the sanctity of life" extend to civilian war casualties? For a while I thought about following Anne Rice and giving up on the Church, while still following Jesus.

According to legend, St. Francis of Assisi once had a vision of the crucified Jesus telling him to rebuild His church. I never had any visions like that (if so, I'd probably check my medication), but I did read something in a book a few years ago that made me rethink things. In one chapter of Margaret Feinberg's book, *The Organic God*, she writes about her struggle with the Church. At the end of the chapter she writes:

> *Now I'm not naive. I realize the church in America is far from perfect and in many ways has gone astray, but the church is still the bride of Christ. She may have holes in her dress, stains on her shoes, and smeared makeup on her face, but at the end of the day, she is still the bride. When we recognize that God's perspective of the church is not necessarily our own, then we will begin treating her with the respect and care she deserves. We will begin building her up to what she is meant to be instead of tearing her down (p. 107-108).*[6]

Ever since I read that passage I have had this nagging feeling that maybe, just maybe, God wants us to *rebuild* the church instead of tear it down. After all, Jesus died for the church, so if he finds it worth redeeming I guess there's still hope.

REBUILDING THE CHURCH

How exactly we go about rebuilding the church, though, is a different story. I'm still trying to figure that one out. However, I can't help but think of the old hymn, "The Church's

---

6   Feinberg, Margaret. *The Organic God*. Grand Rapids: Zondervan, 2007.

One Foundation is Jesus Christ, Her Lord." Notice how the hymn doesn't say that the church's one foundation is penal substitutionary atonement, or the virgin birth, or even the Bible. The foundation of the church is the person of Jesus, the Word-made-flesh. Once the church reestablishes Jesus as its chief cornerstone, maybe then it will truly be the Body of Christ on earth. The church can once again be the hands and feet of Jesus bringing healing to a wounded world.

It's worth a shot, right?

CHAPTER 32
JUMPER CABLES

By Mary C. M. Phillips

I have a love/hate relationship with Dodge Challengers.

When I was ten years old, my mother had acquired one from my uncle. It was a 1974 brown, mean, and masculine-looking model with glittery brown paint that sparkled in the sun.

Today, I'd be more than happy to own a Dodge Challenger or even an old Mustang. Whoever designed these cars had style. Certainly, they are gas-guzzlers in their truest form and completely environmentally unsound automobiles for today, but in terms of style, the Challenger was fierce, (particularly, next to my current blue Town & Country minivan which is shameful in terms of style).

Dickie, my mom's youngest brother had given us the car as he was buying himself a new, sleek convertible. He was in his twenties, had a head of deep red hair, and was always ready with a joke. He listened to Three Dog Night and Led Zeppelin and had all the best records in his collection. Having his old car—or his old anything—was something special!

We welcomed the car as we were in need of a lift (no pun intended). It had been a difficult year to say the least.

A CHALLENGING YEAR

My father had left the family and we were feeling the residual emotions of abandonment. Being the 70s, divorce was uncommon and I felt the pangs of humiliation amongst friends.

When people asked where my father was, I had no answer. Even more embarrassing was when they actually knew his whereabouts—he was usually drunk and very public about it.

The Challenger lifted my spirits and it got our family to-and-fro. It ran perfectly fine—for a while. But as time went by, things began to break.

It got stuck in middle of road. It needed a jump. It overheated. Our hard-earned money went to sleazy mechanics who took advantage of the "divorced woman." Slowly, but surely, our family's bank account disappeared and we slipped into debt.

But we had no other choice. My mother kept putting money into the car since we didn't have the resources to invest in a new one and we were grateful when it had its good days.

A SUNDAY DRIVE

On one particular Sunday morning, we prepared ourselves for church. I made sure not to wear my short-shorts and put double chrome barrettes in my hair so as to appear neat.

I opened the passenger door of the Challenger and sat beside my mom.

"We need a jump," my mother said looking frustrated behind the steering wheel. The battery had lost its charge and the engine was not turning over. It wasn't the first time. As I said, I have a love/hate relationship with Challengers. This was a hate day.

"I can't take it anymore," she said. She had worked late the prior night and looked worn-out. All the long hours of work were catching up to her. My father, in his condition, was unable to pay child support—let alone his own bills. Like so many other families you see every day, we were hurting.

We sat silently in the car thinking of options. Then a ray of sunshine seemed to appear. Right up the block, we saw the neighbors coming out of their house. They too were going to church! What a stroke of luck!

The parents got into their car and waited as their daughter in her pretty dress and white shoes sprang from the house followed by the youngest son, hair still wet, who busied himself closing the door tightly.

"Run, Mary," my mom said with an air of optimism. "Ask Tom (the dad) if he could give us a jump. I'll get the cables out."

I sprinted (as fast as my yellow flip-flops would allow) up the block, along the sidewalk, waving happily to the parked car and asked the younger boy if his dad would help us start our car. I watched him bend his small frame into the car window as a short conversation ensued.

He turned to me and said in a dismissive tone, "We have to get to church. We don't want to be late." He then opened the back door of his car, got inside, and they drove away.

I walked back to our car, as my mom waited. I remember her eyes meeting mine through the windshield. She looked rattled. What had I done wrong? As I sat down in the passenger seat, I conveyed what had happened.

Then she started to cry.

I didn't understand what could have stirred-up such a reaction until she finally said, "Church? What are they learning there?"

It was probably my first taste of irony and false righteousness.

I could not understand how a family with such resources would not help my mother. And why had they had not offered to take us along with them to church, as we attended the same one?

It was not long after this that we stopped going to church altogether.

GOING BACK TO CHURCH

Years later though, with minor scars now healed (one being that my father gave up alcohol after a ten-year battle), I am a churchgoer.

It's a charismatic church (admittedly with a great worship team), but there are all types of people there. All of us have one thing in common: we are imperfect.

People will disappoint you. They always do. Like used-cars, they will let you down. But I've lowered my expectation of people because only Christ is perfect.

Getting together once a week to praise the One who will never let me down is completely worth my time.

Today, on this particular Sunday, I may miss church. Why? There is family down the block with two young children who just lost their mother to cancer. I promised myself to bring them cold cuts from the deli every so often, and I have it on my heart that today is one of those days.

I'll get to church a bit late — or might have to miss a service this week.

I'm going to be the "jumper-cables" for this family today, letting God's love and compassion work through me in order to help them move past the hurt, enabling them to get unstuck. They will in turn enable me to not "go" to church, but "be" the church today.

CHAPTER 33
BEING ON MISSION TOGETHER

By Bill Reichart

Three words bring fear and a sense of failure to the ears of many pastors: "We are leaving." Having served as a local pastor of a small church plant, I know how those words can devastate a young and tender church start up. In 2005 I had just joined the staff of a small, yet growing, church plant just outside of Atlanta. I was given the role of "Assimilation Pastor." Of course, no one in his or her right mind would have ever used that label or title publically — given that the word assimilation appears to the outsider as being cold and manipulative. Therefore my title was packaged differently. I was called the "Pastor of Connecting and Small Groups," which eventually was changed to "Pastor of Doing Life Together." Regardless of my title, my role and responsibilities were the same. I was to make sure first-time visitors felt welcomed and cared for on Sunday mornings. In addition, I was tasked to navigate new people through the steps of the "assimilating" them into the church by helping them find a place to serve, getting them involved in a small group, and eventually helping them become members of the church.

It was a huge task. A task that had as much failure as it did success. The failure often came in the form of either people telling me directly they were leaving or simply choosing to fade away never to return. Those that did tell me they were leaving had a unique story to share but in each story a common theme resonated throughout — people just didn't feel connected to a real and authentic community.

Just several months into my new role at the church, I was pulled aside by an older couple, John and Dottie. They felt they could confide in me because I was new and thought I would have "fresh eyes" to see their concerns. Although this couple served actively and were strategically involved with the church from the very beginning, they felt they needed to move on. They told me that the church felt more like a fast-moving train, and the leadership seemed focused on growth, rather than helping the church function as a family. They told me they felt more like cogs in an engine than people who cared for and connecting with others. My heart broke for John and Dottie because I could hear the cry of their heart. They wanted and expected more from the church. They longed for deep and abiding relationships and community. This was not a good start for me as the new "Assimilation Pastor." After just beginning, people were beginning to jump ship rather than stay on. I wasn't feeling very successful.

The story of John and Dottie wasn't the only story I heard with this similar theme. A couple of years later, a man named Brad, who became a very dear friend of mine at the church, couldn't any longer reconcile being a part of our church. Even though we found a friendship together like that of David and Jonathan in the Bible, he couldn't find any sense of deeper community within the church at large beyond our friendship. He felt that the church wasn't a place where he could *really* know and be known by others. "Doing life together, connecting, and finding community" had become mere slogans of the church but not deep, abiding values and realities that he experienced. What disappointed me was discovering that it required more than just our friendship to keep him connected. It required a larger community—and the larger community failed to reach out to him in a meaningful way.

Simply put, our church had a problem with building community. This is a struggle in most churches, and most try to solve this problem the same way: with small groups. Our church was no different. Very early in my ministry there, I ventured into developing a small group program for our church. Yet I soon discovered that building community through a program of small groups was not going to be an easy and simple solution.

Right from the start we had one group of people, which became deeply committed to each other. They did life together. Actually they did life together too well. Their small group became a clique. At first we did not understand what was going on. We sent newcomers to visit their small group, believing that it would be an inviting place for them to connect. Unfortunately, new people who visited the group never returned to the small group, or to church. Once we recognized the clique for what it was, our task shifted from sending people to the group to attempting to isolate and quarantine the group so that its unhealthy community and practices wouldn't infect others.

A PROBLEM BIGGER THAN JUST OUR BACKYARD

While it may have felt justified to think that those in our church were alone in facing this problem of connection and community—the truth is we weren't alone. The unhappiness with the church "experience" far outstripped our tiny little church and it took those within my Internet community to help me see that reality more clearly.

In addition to my work as a local pastor, I also own and edit a blog called MinistryBestPractices.com. It is a website dedicated to connecting and equipping ministry leaders through practical articles and resources. Over the years, I've posted articles entitled, "Why You Should Leave Your Church," "How to Leave Your Church and Do It Well" and "Five Things to Consider before Leaving Your Church." I posted many of these articles to help ministry leaders and those in the church cope with the epidemic problem of dissatisfaction and people leaving the church. The articles on the subject of leaving the church receive the most comments and questions from readers. Many of the comments come from broken and genuinely hurt people who find themselves confused and disenchanted with the church.

A woman named K. B. added this comment to one of my posts:

> *My husband and I are leaving our current church simply for lack of community. We are one of the few young married couples w/o kids (we are newlyweds) and we've tried this whole year to build*

> up friendships with very little success. Our pastors have a lot invested in us and we love them dearly, and leaving this church really does feel like a terrible break-up. WE want it to work oh-so-badly, but it just isn't working.

The comment from K. B. reflects much of the frustration with the local church. People go to church, and are served by the many programs—but there seems to be a lack of deep, abiding relationships within the church.

DECODING THE PROBLEM

What I've heard in my conversations from John, Dottie, Brad, and K.B are typical of the frustrations with the church "experience." People are struggling to find real and meaningful relationships at church. Because of this struggle, they are dissatisfied and discontent with church. As I listen to people explain their reasons why they weren't connecting with the church, I become confused and frustrated. I tell them that we had small groups and they should get involved in one. But as already pointed out, these small groups sometimes caused more problems than they fixed. I'd mention to them our numerous activities and programs. I would mention that our church had countless touch-points throughout the week where they could meet people, have fellowship, and build relationships.

With all of this, I would put the problem back on them. I'd say to myself, "They just weren't trying." I'd think that they weren't availing themselves of the opportunities before them. Perhaps they just weren't willing to risk knowing new people and being known by them. Although some those statements may have represented for some the reasons why they weren't connecting—holding on to them as the complete answer was missing the point. There was more going on and it wasn't their problem. It was our problem, the problem of the church.

CHURCH IS A MESS, BUT IT'S STILL CHRIST'S

Even though the church may have a plethora of problems and dysfunctions, I still remain connected and a part of it. Why? Because regardless of the junk, messiness and dysfunction—the fact still remains that the church is Christ's. And because I love Christ, I love his church as well. Paul punctuates that point in his letter to the Ephesians:

> So then you are no longer strangers and aliens, but you are fellow citizens with the saints and members of the household of God, built on the foundation of the apostles and prophets, Christ Jesus himself being the cornerstone, in whom the whole structure, being joined together, grows into a holy temple in the Lord. In him you also are being built together into a dwelling place for God by the Spirit (Eph 2:19-22 – ESV).

Helping people discover how the church can be a place of life and growth isn't just predicated on my need to get a paycheck and ensure job security—I believe that it is God's ordained means to build his Kingdom. Nonetheless, I am often frustrated as a pastor with the cultural barnacles and baggage that have attached them to the church. Too often I have felt as if I was functioning as a spiritual "cruise director" catering to the whims and needs of the people rather than pushing God's people into the real and authentic ways of experiencing God and his church.

AIMING AT THE WRONG THING

The problem is that the church has too often gotten it backwards. We've been aiming at the wrong thing. At our church we were attempting to cultivate fellowship, community, and meaningful Christ-centered relationships as an end in themselves. However, that approach will often fails. It's a dead end. In contrast, I began to notice a difference when Christians focused their energy toward serving others—when they were embarking on a "mission together." When God's people gathered with a purpose and mission greater than themselves—it created an environment that bonded the group and developed deep and abiding relationships. Beyond just developing connected relationships, being on mission together also does so much more—it deepens and strengthens our own faith. When we are on mission together we stop chasing after spiritual growth like a consumer trying to get the next spiritual fix. Being on mission and serving others forces us to go deep into our faith and connect intimately with others because we're constantly going to the very precipice of trust and dependence.

When we are on mission together — the ethos and the culture of the church changes. We become less focused on our habit of developing cliques, and instead we become a welcoming church — expecting and anticipating others to join us. When we are on mission together, even our prayers change. We become less focused on merely praying for our own needs but instead we pray Kingdom prayers of seeing lives and communities transformed by the gospel.

Having begun to understand this while serving at the church, we created mission as the center of our church. Therefore small groups didn't just gather for "gathering sake" — they were purposed and had a mission to serve. Repurposing our church's focus and energy outward toward mission and service, created a healthier church and a people of God who were becoming growing Disciples of Christ. Church isn't broken; rather many of the forms and cultural expectations we've created around it are. The church can recapture God's ordained purpose and capture the hearts of lives of its people, when it becomes a gathered and sent people who embark on mission together.

CHAPTER 34
I HATE THE CHURCH. I LOVE THE CHURCH.

By Aubry G. Smith

The day my brother died is the day the church began to fail me.

I revisit that day often. I can still hear my father's voice on the phone: "Something's happened with Tripp. You need to come *now*." He gave no details about my older brother, but his voice quivered with emotion. My father never shows emotion. My brain went into a fog, and I have only the faintest memory of my roommate packing my clothes and my fiancé driving me across the state.

When we got to the hospital, I finally got the details. Tripp was in a coma. He had been experimenting with drugs, and two had interacted and stopped his breathing for nearly an hour. Lifeless tubes now breathed for him. I held his cold hand, and looked into his half-opened eyes that seemed as if they might, at any moment, turn to look at me. The doctors told us that we were only waiting for him to die. Over the next several hours, his vital signs went through numerous cycles of crashing and then steadying. I prayed all through the night that he would come out of the coma.

The next morning, Tripp's wife made the agonizing decision to turn off the machines.

Papers were signed.

Tripp was dead.

I went back to my life in my Christian huddle, but I was suddenly disconnected from everyone. Cards poured in, promising that Tripp was "in a better place" or that "God needed another angel." No one knew what to say to me. "If it makes you feel any better, my grandpa died last year. I know just how you feel." Most said nothing at all; afraid I would break down before them. As time went on, I distanced myself more and more.

Those in the church carefully avoided eye contact with me, maneuvering around me to avoid the black hole that I was becoming.

THE DEATH OF CHURCH

The nightmares came slowly at first. Replays of happy past events with Tripp turned into horrific deaths. One dream began with laughing at an inside joke with my mom, but ended with me turning in a rage and stabbing Tripp in the chest with a knife. I dreamt of standing as a bridesmaid on his wedding day with everyone smiling, but then the pastor pulled a gun out of his Bible and shot Tripp in the head.

Such dreams came nightly and turned more frightening as the weeks went on. I was haunted by demonic, yellow eyes set in beautiful, dark bodies that told stories of Tripp's death in ever more graphic and grotesque ways. I often woke up and tried to scream, but felt as if someone was sitting on my chest, holding my throat.

My eyes developed dark circles and I became emotionally distant. Somehow, everyone thought I was coping just fine. They rarely asked, and never listened. Without ever needing to answer that question for others, I eventually forgot to ask it of myself. I spiraled deeper into my grief. Church became a tomb for me, holding my fallen and dead notions of community.

The church was dead to me.

Over the next three years, I struggled to stay in the church. I hoped no one would ask about my hollow spiritual and emotional state, but I also mourned that no one ever did. Those who had once asked what God was doing in my heart, now avoided even asking if I was doing well today. I saw, perhaps for the first time, that Christians loved to talk about love, hope, and joy, but almost never about suffering, grief, or depression. In a sermon, one pastor even claimed that Christians couldn't experience depression because the Holy Spirit doesn't allow it.

I pushed further away from Christians. How could I have real relationships with people who don't believe in suffering? How could I connect with anyone who has never been in the cavernous darkness I was in?

I married Brady three weeks after my brother's death, and perhaps my husband's job as a worship leader was the only thing dragging me to the worship gatherings on Sunday mornings and to small group. I rarely participated in our small group discussions, and when I did, I wielded a cutting remark about all the Christian failings. I settled into cynicism, reveling in every mistake the church made. I was angry by day and terrified by night.

LOVING THE CHURCH

A year after Tripp's death, I had a different sort of dream.

I was at a concert—noisy, intrusive, and blinding—so I sought refuge backstage. My friend David was waiting for me, and handed me a newspaper. The headlines on the paper were splashed with all of my past pain: "Mom Diagnosed with Brain Tumors! Parents Divorce! Family Broken! Brother Dies! Depression and Loneliness!" Sobs racked my body. I lowered my arms to drop the heavy paper. Then David placed a ball of bread dough, of all things, on the newspaper covering all the headlines.

Somehow I knew in my subconscious self exactly what it meant: the dough was Christ's broken body. His body is given for us. He is a God who suffers with us. Who suffers with *me*? But the dough of my dream had not yet risen and was unbaked—unfinished, just like the church, the body of Christ. Though imperfect, she is a minister of Christ in this world—fumbling, and often failing—but a minister of Christ nonetheless.

It was time for me to wake up, and to begin the hard work of loving the church again.

My husband prayed relentlessly for the nightmares to stop, and they eventually did. The dark circles faded from my eyes, and I slowly revived. I prayed for the ability to move beyond my own pain and truly care for other Christians. I prayed for those who had said careless things to me, or who had avoided me when they should have wept with me. I prayed for my ability to pray, because I didn't have the strength to even do that. In small group, I tried to identify things that the church was doing right, rather than remaining sullen and critical.

You would think that as my attitude toward the church changed toward love, my experience of church would also change. But it didn't. I was burned again. And again. And again.

I hate the church.

But part of me can't stop loving the church.

There have been those who have genuinely cared for me, saying the wrong things when they didn't know what the right words were, but trying to offer comfort anyway. There were anonymous gifts of cash in unmarked envelopes when the recession hit and there were no jobs and rent was due the next day. There is an older couple who loves my family as if we were their own children, taking our children as their adopted grandchildren and praying for us daily. My in-laws have revealed Christ to me; loving me as a true daughter and supporting me in ways my biological family could not.

When a friend of mine lost his hands in an electrical accident, I saw the church rush to love his family. There were always at least five people from the church in the hospital, but usually there were so many that the nurses grew frustrated. There was ongoing, fervent prayer. There were shared tears. There were abundant meals. Their three children were cared for so that his wife could stay at the hospital full-time. The church pooled tens of thousands of dollars in a poor country community to support the family's lost income. This is the church that I love. This is the body of Christ.

LACK OF MATURITY

I believe that the wounds I carry from life in the church come, in large part, from a lack of maturity. We have an abundance of Bible studies on any topic, but there are few older believers showing younger believers how to live in faith—how to *be* the church. Few people know how to sit in a waiting room with a horror on the other side of the wall, holding the hand of a shaken wife or a wailing friend, how to sit at a grave in silent but full presence with the grieving, or to voice the "How Long, O Lord?" prayers for those who despair but can't find the words themselves. Few know how to open their wallets or kitchens freely, sacrificially meeting needs.

How can Christians know how to be like Christ, if they have no one to imitate—someone to bring flesh to the words of the Bible?

Being like Jesus is bearing the sufferings of others, walking with them in death and doubt, nightmares and lost hope. So I invite teenagers into my home to pray, study Scripture together, and talk about their tangled and confused lives. I push them for deeper conversations and going beyond the "I'm-just-fine-how-are-you" response, because these hard talks were what I needed in my darkest times. I sit with Christians and share what God is doing in my life, how I see the little pieces coming together, and voicing my frustrations when I can't see the shape that the pieces are taking.

Rubbing shoulders with the sinners-being-made-saints of the church has changed me. Having been hurt by them, I am quicker to repent of my own sins that harm others. Having been ignored, I am more careful to reach out to others in pain. Having suffered alone, I suffer with those who suffer. I find that the hardship of being in the church is also, in some wild way, a method that Jesus uses to make us more like Him.

The years that I grudgingly went to church were not wasted years. While the indifference or awkwardness of some Christians fueled my anger, the Scripture spoken there pushed me into faith when I was most resistant. I watched a young widow serve others selflessly, still full of pain but moving forward in love, and I longed for that strength. I saw others genuinely worship when I couldn't bear to, and in some ways, I feel that they carried me along with them, resuscitating me and bringing me back into worship. Staying in the church brought me back to life.

Jesus plans to resurrect the church, to finish baking that bread. I see glimpses of that Resurrection-hope in the good ways that the church loves, but it is hard work pushing away the ashes to see it.

CHAPTER 35
FOCUSING ON PEOPLE

By John Walker

"If we're going to grow, we need a new sanctuary," our pastor proclaimed. We met with architects and contractors, who drew plans and figured costs. We had plenty of land, but unfortunately, not lots of money. We could not afford to build the new sanctuary we had envisioned.

FOCUSING ON THE BUILDING

We went with Plan Two—build the fellowship center first, a large building itself, but smaller and less costly than a new sanctuary. We planned to use that building as a sanctuary until we could afford to build the larger building. Financing the fellowship center was a stretch for our congregation, since interest on our loan in those days of a heady economy was pegged at fourteen percent. Nevertheless, based on the church's income, we decided we could make the payments. We built the fellowship center.

During the following years however, the economy softened. Almost one-fifth of the families in our congregation depended on the construction business for their incomes. Over a two year period, all but two of those families lost their source of income and left the area to find work elsewhere. The church's income declined. The payments on the loan for the fellowship center began consuming a huge portion of the church's income. Soon the church owed almost forty thousand dollars that we did not have.

"What can we do?" we asked ourselves. "We don't have the money and we don't know where to get it."

The leadership and the congregation were discouraged. Not only was the church in financial trouble, but many of the families in the congregation were also struggling financially. Would we lose our sanctuary/fellowship center? Would we lose our homes?

FOCUSING ON PEOPLE

In spite of our discouragement, we felt the Spirit leading us to focus on people—people in the congregation as well as people in the community. One couple began a "cookie ministry" to people who visited the church. Every local visitor received a plate of homemade cookies the week after their visit.

Some of our members realized that the churches in our community rarely cooperated on much of anything. The Easter Sunrise service, where several pastors each took turns leading parts of the service, appeared to be the primary annual cooperative effort between churches. Some churches never participated in even that event.

A well-known Christian film series was released. Since our new fellowship center was the largest building in the entire community, we offered to host the showing of the series, and personally invited every church in the community to be involved. Every church accepted the invitation and participated. That was a first for our community.

One church in the community wanted to host an internationally known missions speaker, but did not have adequate facilities to accommodate the event. Even though that church and ours did not see eye-to-eye doctrinally, we offered our facility for the event, and hosted and prepared the banquet that accompanied it.

This new spirit of cooperation among the churches attracted the attention of the community, which noticed that the churches were getting along with each other in Christian love. That benefitted every church in the community. People who previously had little interest in church decided to see what had changed. People visited the churches, and some found a church home.

Others in our church noticed the lack of contact between people in the congregation during the week and started "Wednesday Night Dinners." For a nominal fee, families could get a homemade dinner, followed by small group Bible studies, children's programs, teen activities, choir practice, just hanging out, and other assorted activities. Within weeks, Wednesday evening attendance almost eclipsed Sunday morning attendance. Most importantly, people who barely knew each other were soon good friends. People who needed others to help shoulder their burdens began finding help.

Home small group Bible studies also proliferated. There were women's groups, men's groups, couple's groups, and teen groups. Without a doubt the most unusual group was a women's group that met at 5:00 AM. You read that correctly. 5:00 AM! 5:00 AM, while children and husbands are still sleeping. As one of the ladies in the group said, "It was either 10:00 PM or 5:00 AM. The earlier time actually works best for us. Everything is quiet and our families are still sleeping." Once again, people built relationships and friendships.

When we get to know each other better, we can choose to close ranks, becoming a tight-knit group that excludes everyone else, or we can choose to open ourselves to new people. Amazingly, most of our groups chose the latter, even though the groups that had been in existence the longest adapted to this new way of thinking more slowly.

DIRTY MONEY

As these groups included more and more new people, the church began to grow. If you're getting ahead of me in the story and have already decided that new people meant new income, which was used to get the church out of debt, you're not exactly correct. Although new people did eventually develop into new sources of income (new people often take several years to decide to give regularly to the church), that did not solve the church's immediate financial needs.

One morning, however, the UPS driver dropped off a small package at the church office. The church secretary opened it and found a plastic container like those used to hold leftover food. Inside she discovered what appeared to be chunks of dirt, wrapped in cloth, in a bed of powder.

How would chunks of dirt solve the church's problems? It turned out that those chunks of dirt contained lots of cash, cash that had obviously been buried in dirt. The amount came to almost the exact amount the church was behind on its bills.

Usually, the United States Treasury Department considers burying money in the dirt and thereby ruining it "defacement," which is illegal. However, if such money is anonymously donated to a charitable organization, such as a church, the Treasury Department will peel apart the dirty, rotten money, count it and send a check for the total amount to the charitable organization. This money, of course, was donated to our church anonymously.

The plastic container of dirty, rotten money got the church back in the black financially, but what did that have to do with focusing on people? Even though I have no proof, I believe I know the source of the money. The church had helped a person in their time of need and now, this person was returning the favor and helping the church.

I have this suspicion because I was part of the team that helped this person out. I still remember getting a call from the pastor. "You've got to be kidding!" I exclaimed. "He's not going to find anyone who can do that."

"You're right," the pastor said. "He has already tried. He can't find anyone. Worse still, it has to be done day-after-tomorrow. You can say no if you want."

As we talked I thought of a possible way to do what needed done. "Let me make some calls and call in some favors and get back to you."

Within a few hours everything was in place and we found a way for the church to pull together some help for our friend. A few weeks later a small package was delivered to the church office. Since the donation was anonymous I will allow it to remain anonymous, except to say that it was almost certainly a result of the church focusing on people.

Because the church helped people, the church paid its bills. In the ensuing years, the church has operated in the black. Today the church has not only the largest building in the community, but also the largest congregation—a thriving congregation that focuses on people.

CHAPTER 36
WE WANT WORSHIP!

By Markus Watson

When I look back, I sometimes wonder, "So... What exactly did I see in this church?" To be honest, I'm still not entirely sure why I agreed to pastor this church. But I'm glad I did.

Northminster Presbyterian Church had been in decline for over twenty years. And the more the church declined, the more people became anxious and antagonistic toward one another. Big arguments broke out over the question, "How do we start to grow again?" Some said, "Let's get a new organ! That'll bring people in." Others said, "You're crazy! We need to focus on contemporary worship."

The "worship wars" were in full swing in our church.

After I interviewed to be their pastor, I started calling the church's references—and I received one negative report after another. One person said, "Markus, some of the people in that church are really hard to work with." A denominational staff person said, "You should know that Northminster is a church in conflict. If things don't get better with the next pastor we're probably going to have to close it down."

Yikes! No pressure, whatsoever.

But I still agreed to be their pastor. Somehow my wife and I felt like this was the church God was calling us to. I started as the pastor of Northminster Presbyterian Church on October 1, 2007.

SERVICE TENSION

I noticed right away the tension between the "Contemporary Service" and the "Heritage Service." The Contemporary Service had an attendance of about 65 people (and growing — slightly) and the Heritage Service had about 45 people (and declining). It was clear to me that it was only a matter of time before the Heritage service wouldn't exist anymore. But I wasn't going to force any changes until the issue was ripe. I firmly believe God speaks through his people, so I was waiting for a cue — from God and from God's people.

That cue came about six months into my time at Northminster in the middle of a Budget and Finance meeting. It was not the timing I expected! Shirley, an older lady, who attended the Heritage Service, is known for saying exactly what she thinks. She does not hold back! At a certain point in the meeting, Shirley jumped in and said, "Can I change the subject?"

"Sure," I said.

"How much longer are we going to keep doing the Heritage Service?"

This was not the question I was expecting from her. *Ok, I thought. Let's see where this conversation goes.* "Well, that's a good question."

Shirley got right to the point. "I mean, how many more people have to die? Ten? Twenty? What's the cutoff?"

I knew this was my cue. The issue was ripe. The congregation was ready to talk about this.

A few weeks later I preached a sermon called "The Truth About Change." The sermon had already been on the calendar (confirmation to me that God was involved), so it was a no-brainer to bring up the issue of going to one service in this sermon. At the end of the service, I asked the congregation to consider the possibility of going to one service that would primarily be contemporary.

"No decisions have been made," I said at the end of my sermon. "All I'm doing today is bringing up the idea. What I want you to do is talk to each other about it. Talk to me about it.

On your way out of church this morning, let me know what you think. Then, in a few weeks, we'll talk it over as a congregation. Only then—after listening to all of you—will the elders make a final decision."

I wasn't surprised by the response of those in the Contemporary Service; they were all for it. What amazed me was the response of those in the Heritage Service. Some said nothing to me and certainly didn't look happy. But more people than I could have imagined said something along the lines of, "Well, I'm not really excited about it, but I think it's what we need to do."

CONGREGATIONAL ADAPTATION

A few weeks later we had a congregational meeting designed to let everyone share his or her thoughts on moving to one service. I'd been told that in the past, congregational meetings had exploded into shouting matches, so I had some anxiety over how this would go.

I'd been reading a book at the time called *Surfing the Edge of Chaos*,[7] a terrific book about how biological organisms adapt to changes in the environment while drawing comparisons to organizations that are able to adapt to changes in their environment. I have to admit I don't remember what it was, but something in that book helped me structure this meeting effectively. I remember being in the shower on Sunday morning as the structure for this meeting came clear for me.

Here's what I did.

With everyone sitting around tables in groups of six to eight people, I gave them some ground rules. First, everyone gets to speak; no one's voice was to be unheard. Second, no one gets to interrupt; each person has a right to say what he or she wants to say. Third, everyone listens.

Then I gave them some instructions. Each table had to elect someone to take notes on what people shared, and a presenter to tell the whole congregation what was shared at their table. Then I provided three questions for discussion:

7 Pascale, Richard, Mark Millemen, and Linda Gioja. *Surfing the Edge of Chaos*. New York: Random House, 2000.

1. What do you love about our church right now?
2. How do you feel about going to one contemporary service?
3. What hopes do you have for Northminster's future?

After about half an hour of sharing around their tables, each presenter came up and shared what they'd talked about at their table. Things were going smoothly until Hal came up to present.

Hal was about 75 years old and had been on the Pastor Nominating Committee that hired me. He was pretty forward-looking for his age, so I was really surprised when he stood up and said, "I wish we could go back to 1970."

I don't know if my face gave away the shock I felt. I thought to myself, "*What?!*"

Then Hal said, "I wish we could sing all of our traditional hymns every week and do all of our traditional liturgy."

Hal! I silently cried. *"What are you doing?!"*

"But we can't go back to 1970."

Whew…

"It's not a matter of *if* we're going to change, it's a matter of *when*. And I say *when is now*."

Wow! The congregation erupted in applause!

But not everyone was happy.

As the next presenter began to share his table's support for going to a single contemporary service, Maggie stood up at her table and in a shrill voice cried out, "We want worship!" The implication was that only traditional worship is true worship.

I stood up immediately and went to the mic. "Maggie, this is a time for sharing and listening." Maggie continued to shout. I said again, "This is a time for sharing and listening." I looked over at the presenter who was clearly a bit stunned by the outburst. This needed to be a safe place for people to share their ideas. Maggie's outburst was making this an unsafe environment, and I couldn't let that happen.

So this time I simply said, "Maggie, this is not appropriate." Maggie continued shouting. Again, "Maggie, this is not appropriate." More shouting, but with a brief glance toward me. Again, more firmly this time and stepping out from behind the mic toward Maggie, "Maggie, this is not appropriate!"

Finally, she stopped. She looked over at me with a slightly defeated look and sat down. I hadn't wanted to "defeat" her, but we needed to set a new pattern for how we relate to each other in this church. Outbursts of anger didn't belong in a community of Jesus-followers. I think that moment was a turning point for Northminster.

After that, the rest of the meeting went smoothly. Clearly, not everyone wanted to lose the Heritage Service, but a vast majority of the congregation was behind the change. The following week, the elders voted to go to one Contemporary Service.

GOD IS AT WORK

I don't tell this story to say that contemporary worship is better than traditional. It's not. I don't tell this story to say that contemporary worship is the solution to declining attendance. It's not.

I tell this story because I was able to see God at work. God spoke through Shirley in that Budget and Finance meeting. God spoke through Hal in the congregational meeting. And, in a way, God spoke through Maggie. Or, at least, God used that moment to establish a new way of relating in our church.

As I look back now, I can hardly believe how much we've changed in the past four years. No, our attendance hasn't skyrocketed. No, contemporary worship wasn't the answer to all our problems.

But we're definitely no longer a dying church! If you want to talk attendance, we've at least stopped the bleeding.

Amazingly, there has been virtually no major conflict at Northminster since that time. Some folks left the church over the change (as expected), and others have come to Northminster since that time. But it's all been peaceful.

Our average age has dropped. We tend to pick up several young families a year. And our children's ministry is growing like nuts!

Don't get me wrong. We're still a long way from being the church God is calling us to be. But we're on the path. And we're doing our best to follow Jesus.

But you know what's really ironic? Two of the key people who influenced this change—Shirley and Hal—no longer attend. You know who's still with us? Maggie!

ABOUT THE CONTRIBUTORS

LEAVING CHURCH

Chapter 1. Lew Ayotte is the author of the blog *The Life of Lew Ayotte* (LewAyotte.com) a collection of stories about philosophy, religion, technology, and everyday life. Lew lives in Athens, GA with his beautiful wife Kati, two children, eight cats, and two dogs.

Chapter 2. Carey Crawford is an adjunct instructor at Dallas Christian College and leads the reGenesis Network, which seeks to begin Missional Communities and train others in the incarnational lifestyle. Carey Crawford holds a Doctor of Ministry degree from Mid-America Baptist Theological Seminary. He writes a blog called *Leaving Church, Inc.*, and his website is YouCanBeginAgain.com.

Chapter 3. Michael Donahoe is 58 years old and lives in central Ohio with Betty, his wife of 21 years. They have five children and 13 grandkids. Michael grew up in the Methodist church and went to several different types of churches before finally realizing that church was not found in a building, but in each of us who are saved by grace. He blogs at DoneWithReligion.com.

Chapter 4. Glenn Hager is a freelance writer, living with his wife, Patty in the Chicago area. He has two adult children, three grandchildren and two great grandchildren. Glenn loves bike riding, wailing on his guitar, traveling, hanging out with friends and family, reading, and writing. He is fond of encouraging people to change the system by making it irrelevant through new, creative options.

Chapter 5. Wayne Hobson is the author of the eBook, *Suffer the Little Children: Understanding and Overcoming Spiritual Abuse* and has been in ministry for over 25 years. He studied theology at Wilberforce and Lincoln Universities. He holds a B.A. in Business from La Salle University in Philadelphia, Pennsylvania, where he also minored in psychology (including counseling techniques). Wayne is a husband and a father of three children—one son and two daughters. Wayne and his wife Dorothy currently reside in North Carolina and he has been a writer for Examiner.com since 2009.

Chapter 6. Judith Huang is a Singaporean writer and editor. A recipient of the Foyle Young Poet of the Year Award in 2001, 2003, and 2004, her poetry has been published in journals and anthologies at home and abroad. She graduated from Harvard University in 2010, where she was elected to the Signet Society of Arts and Letters. Visit her portfolio at www.judithhuang.com.

Chapter 7. Mike Keffer works full-time in the financial services industry. He lives in southern West Virginia with his wife of 25 years who is a homemaker. Together they raise two sons, one of them autistic and the other gifted. All four of them love Jesus.

Chapter 8. A former worship pastor who grew up in the church, Travis Klassen has seen a lot from "the inside," and is currently writing a book about his experiences. Travis's blog can be found at www.churchburned.com. Travis lives life with his soul mate, Brandee, and their two daughters in Vancouver, BC, Canada.

Chapter 9. Tyson Phillips grew up in the Midwest and now he and his family live on the West Coast.

Chapter 10. Tara Pohlkotte currently tells her stories of life, as she discovers it, at her personal blog: www.pohlkottepress.com. She is also a contributing author for another current Civitas Press title: *Soul Bare: Reflections on Becoming Human.* Holding a BA in Psychology and pursuing her Masters in Marriage and Family Therapy, Tara lives and works in Appleton, Wisconsin with her husband and two children. She loves to read, play cards, dance wildly, people watch, scribble poetry on the back of coloring pages, and spend the weekends in sweatpants with her family.

Chapter 11. Will Rochow currently works in a Catholic healthcare facility, where, besides his regular duties, he also has many pastoral care opportunities that he enjoys. Will is also a licensed semi-trailer driver and occasionally is still asked to do some relief trucking. Some of Will's many hobbies include motorcycling, wine making, reading, blogging, and cooking. Will lives with his wife Ginny in Lethbridge, Alberta. They have two adult children.

Chapter 12. Brian Swan is the author of a blog called *Allergic to BS,* a collection of stories about life within the walls of an institutional church. Brian Swan lives in Crestwood, KY with his wife Kristin, and his two children, Emrick and Carley. Brian loves to race BMX bikes, and is occasionally found off-roading in his 1993 Toyota Land cruiser.

Chapter 13. Genevieve Thul is the author of *Turquoise Gates* (TurquoiseGates.com), a blog about her battle with cancer and the faith transformation it's birthed in the past four years. She is a contributing author at Dayspring's faith blog, Incourage.me. Genevieve is in her mid-30s and lives in rural Wisconsin with her husband and four kids. She is currently in the final stages of Ph.D. dissertation work online, and she and her family are searching for a healthy church to call home.

SWITCHING CHURCH

Chapter 14. Shannon Brisco is the Program Officer for a non-profit integral mission organization. She has her bachelor of administration from Tyndale University and her masters of arts in international development from Eastern University. She speaks Spanish and loves to travel, cook, and spend time with her family.

Chapter 15. Jessica Bowman married her high-school sweetheart when she was 17 years old. Together, they are raising four children. She blogs at bohemianbowmans.com and is the author of *Parenting Wild Things – Embracing the Rumpus.* She loves writing, hooping, and theology.

Chapter 16. Lauren LaRue attended Douglas Anderson School of Performing Arts during several years of high school, and is currently working on her Bachelors of Science and Psychology. She is a mother and a wife, and an advocate to the broken hearted. Laura enjoys reading, writing, and meditating in her spare time.

Chapter 17. Kellen Freeman is a writer living with his wife in Ohio. He is a graduate from the Methodist Theological School in Ohio with a Master of Theological Studies. He blogs regularly about the intersection of life and faith at KellenFreeman.net.

You can also find him on Twitter @kellenfreeman. Kellen is currently writing his first book.

Chapter 18. Eric Hatfield trained as a Civil Engineer, and worked in environment protection and watershed management until he retired. He lives in Sydney, Australia and enjoys reading, contemporary music, travel, the World Wide Web (he has a website and two blogs), the stimulating company of young people, and (most of all) spending time with his wife.

Chapter 19. Wayne Hobson is the author of the e-book, *Suffer the Little Children: Understanding and Overcoming Spiritual Abuse* and has been in ministry for over 25 years. He studied theology at Wilberforce and Lincoln Universities. He holds a B.A. in Business from La Salle University in Philadelphia, Pennsylvania, where he also minored in psychology (including counseling techniques). Wayne is a husband and a father of three children—one son and two daughters. Wayne and his wife Dorothy currently reside in North Carolina and he has been a writer for Examiner.com since 2009.

Chapter 20. Kimberly Parker is author of *Radical Love... Forever Changed*, a book that identifies the misconceptions about God's love and guides the reader to experiencing more of it (RadicalLoveBook.com). You can connect with her through her website, SimplyCreativeWriting.com, where she provides writing and speaking services for businesses, ministries and individuals across the globe.

Chapter 21. Felisa Reed has her Bachelor of Arts degree in Anthropology and Intercultural Studies with a minor in Bible. As this is a rather unmarketable degree, she currently travels the country working at various Renaissance festivals.

Chapter 22. Sam Riviera has written the series "Getting to Know Your Neighbors" and "Being the Church" on the GraceGround blog. Sam and his wife are retired and live in San Diego, California.

Chapter 23. Cara Sexton is a wife, mother, foster parent, blogger, decorator, writer, and wannabe artist who finds her peace in a variety of creative undertakings and strives to encourage others on their faith journeys. She aims to live out loud with grace and gusto and invites you to do the same over at her blog, WhimsySmitten.com. Watch for her upcoming book, *Soul Bare: Reflections on Becoming Human*, due out from Civitas Press in the spring of 2013.

REFORMING CHURCH

Chapter 24. For over 30 years Alan Brisco was a consultant to multi-national corporate clients. In 2010, he founded The Cornerstone Community, a ministry serving those who influence change or transition in Christian contexts. Alan authors the blog, *Wisdom for a Change*. He produces and hosts the interview-format podcast, *Provoked to Newness*.

Chapter 25. Kris Camealy is a homeschooling mother of four. She serves as an advocate for Compassion International, a MOPS coordinator, and encourager to many, while maintaining her personal blog, AlwaysAlleluia.com. Her writing has been featured at Incourage.me and she serves as a contributor to *Five Minutes for Faith*. In her spare time she reads, runs and plays with her camera. She is a contributing author to the upcoming project, *Soul Bare* due out in March 2013.

Chapter 26. Daniel Darling is the Senior Pastor of Gages Lake Bible Church in the northwest suburbs of Chicago and is the author of several books, including his latest, *Real, Owning Your Christian Faith*. His work has been featured by a variety of evangelical publications such as "Relevant Magazine," "Focus on the Family," and "Christianity Today." He regularly blogs at DanielDarling.com. He is a sought after-speaker and is often interviewed on television and radio. He and his wife, Angela, have four children.

Chapter 27. Melody Harrison Hanson was a contributor to *Not Alone* and *Not Afraid*, other community projects by Civitas Press. She also blogs quietly at LogicAndImagination.com, where she tries to use her power for good. It is the messy musings of a feminist, believer & doubter, mother, alcoholic, sometimes melancholic, photographer, poet, and writer. Forgiven and grateful, she lives in Madison, WI with her husband and four kids, two cats, a dog, and oodles of dust mites.

Chapter 28. Dan King is the author of *The Unlikely Missionary: From Pew-Warmer to Poverty-Fighter,* the story about how a trip to Africa turned one man's world upside down and changed everything he knew about Christianity. The book has received recognition and high commendations from his mom, his wife, and his children (We're still hoping for an endorsement from Tim Tebow). Dan lives in Sarasota, FL with his wife and two kids.

Chapter 29. Alan Knox is the publisher of "The Assembling of the Church" at AlanKnox.net. He lives with his wife and two children just north of Raleigh, North Carolina. He enjoys spending time with his family and friends, web development, and running.

Chapter 30. Sonny Lemmons blogs at LookThrough.net, sharing thoughts on faith and fatherhood. He left a 13-year career in Higher Education Administration to become a full-time stay-at-home dad (to Kai, 3) and husband (to Ashley, perfect). Sonny was a contributing author to *The Myth of Mr. Mom* (Portmanteau Press, 2011) and *Not Afraid* (Civitas Press, forthcoming).

Chapter 31. Travis Mamone is the co-host of the weekly podcast "Something Beautiful." He has written for such publications as "Provoketive Magazine," "Relevant Magazine," "Burnside Writers Collective," and "The Upper Room." He has also contributed to the books *Not Alone: Stories of Living with Depression* (Civitas Press, 2011) and *Not Afraid: Stories of Finding Significance* (Civitas Press, 2012). He lives in Easton, MD, and blogs at TravisMamone.net.

Chapter 32. Mary C. M. Phillips is a caffeinated wife, mother, and writer of short stories and personal essays. Her work has appeared in numerous *Cup of Comfort* and *Chicken Soup for the Soul* anthologies. She blogs at CaffeineEpiphanies.wordpress.com.

Chapter 33. Bill Reichart is an ordained pastor in the Presbyterian Church in America and is currently serving as the Atlanta area director for the Christian Medical and Dental Associations. Bill also owns and edits a blog called

MinistryBestPractices.com, which is designed and dedicated to equip church leaders for innovative ministry.

Chapter 34. Aubry Smith is a freelance writer and stay-at-home mom to her two toddler boys. Aubry is an Arkansas native transplanted in Raleigh, North Carolina, where she and her husband are training for ministry. When not wrestling with her babies or writing, she enjoys reading, cooking, hiking, and camping.

Chapter 35. John Walker and his wife are retired and enjoy gardening, walking their dogs, and cooking.

Chapter 36. Markus Watson is the pastor of Northminster Presbyterian Church in San Diego, California. He is currently working toward a Doctor of Ministry degree at Fuller Theological Seminary in the area of Missional Leadership, studying under Alan Roxburgh and Mark Lau Branson. Markus blogs on issues of missional leadership at MarkusWatson.com and has published film reviews for the quarterly journal, *Visual Parables*. Markus lives in San Diego with his wife, Robin, and three children. He loves surfing and sci-fi.

www.ingramcontent.com/pod-product-compliance
Lightning Source LLC
Chambersburg PA
CBHW060514100426
42743CB00009B/1305